the
teen owner's
manual

the
teen
owner's manual

OPERATING INSTRUCTIONS, TROUBLESHOOTING TIPS, AND ADVICE ON ADOLESCENT MAINTENANCE

by Sarah Jordan, with Janice Hillman, M.D.

Illustrated by Paul Kepple and Scotty Reifsnyder

QUIRK BOOKS
PHILADELPHIA

Library of Congress Cataloging in Publication Number: 2009929778

ISBN: 978-1-59474-417-4
Printed in China
Typeset in Swiss

Designed and illustrated by Paul Kepple and Scotty Reifsnyder @ Headcase Design
www.headcasedesign.com
Production management by John J. McGurk

Distributed in North America by Chronicle Books
680 Second Street
San Francisco, CA 94107

10 9 8 7 6 5 4 3 2 1

Quirk Books
215 Church Street
Philadelphia, PA 19106
www.quirkbooks.com

Contents

Welcome

to your new role as parent of a teenager!

Congratulations on making it this far as a parent.

We've all heard the refrain: "Just you wait until your kid becomes a teenager! Then you'll be in for it." These scare-mongering tactics are pretty effective at spooking parents who are about to go through the teen years for the first time. Vague and doom-filled cautionary tales and whispered warnings produce chills down most parents' spines largely because we aren't precisely sure what we are "in for"—or if we are ready.

But it only takes a brief walk down memory lane and recollection of our own youthful indiscretions to give us pause. Moms and dads can regale one another for hours with stories of sneaking out second-floor windows to get to that forbidden party, strategic omissions of who would be driving to a concert in order to get permission to attend, getting drunk on cheap wine with friends in the confines of sheltering rhododendron bushes, getting hot and heavy with the lifeguard under the boardwalk, sophisticated ways to hold the cigarette, seeing how many friends you could jam into a car, cranking up the radio and singing at the top of our lungs till we got to the mall....

Oh yes, we parents have had plenty of this type of nostalgic, slightly foolish (or totally reckless) adventures. But now we are the ones staying up late chewing our fingernails waiting for our son to come home from his first party with the guys on the varsity soccer team, or driving white-knuckled for a meeting with the principal about suspected cheating, or having to make small talk with our daughter's prom date while we wait for her to emerge from her room in all of her blossoming beauty.

Our parents somehow got us through the teen years. But do we know what to do to guide our own kids? In these very different times? Parents may be tempted to go into serious lock-down on their teen's freedoms and micromanage a son or daughter's every move. But that would be wrong. A teen's job during these years is to separate from the parental cocoon and establish his or her own autonomy and self reliance.

Our job is to prepare our growing boy or girl for young adulthood, which will be coming soon enough. That means active and engaged parenting with plenty of compassion, communication, limit setting and thoughtful guidance. This book offers practical information on just how to do this.

The teen years are bewildering to both child and parent. Your teen's mood swings, morphing body, hormone surges, complex and volatile social world, and drive for independence can really make parents feel clueless. All we ever want to do is help as our teens figure out this process of growing up. In this manual, we have divided the teen experience into seven chapters.

Cram Session: Prepping for the Teen Years (pages 20–39) reviews the teen's basic drives and motivations to explain her changing behavior. It also details basic parenting dos and don'ts to support your teen through her transformation.

Physical Education: The Changing Body and Mind of Your Teen (pages 40–99) breaks down the timing of puberty and describes what to expect during each stage. You'll learn about teen hygiene, sleep, and body image; what daughters want to know about breast development and menstruation; and what sons want to know about changing penile behavior.

School Daze: Managing Academic Life (pages 100–129) looks at how to manage such hot-button issues as homework, stress, and college admission prep.

Social Studies: Your Teen's Scene (pages 130–165) explains how boys and girls differ in matters of love, and what parents need to know about crushes, dating, break-ups, hook-ups, and meddling in your teen's romantic life. This chapter also addresses the age-old concerns about how to give The Sex Talk and impart advice on birth control and sexual orientation.

Language Requirement: The Importance of Communication (pages 166–185) teaches you strategies for talking to your teen. It explains how to defuse raging or silent teens, how to handle bad language, and how to recognize the signs of teen depression.

Pep Rally: Limit-Testing and Independence (pages 186–207) discusses discipline and punishment, why kids take risks, and what to say to your teen about alcohol and substance abuse. This chapter also explains how to prep your teen for a party (and when to crash one); how to help your teen confront peer pressure; and even how to teach your child to drive.

Graduation: Flying the Coop and Beyond (pages 208–215) recaps the journey you and your teen have completed and what to expect now. It also reviews how to handle your emotions once your child has left home, and what to do about a child who continues to live at home long after high school graduation.

Teens are starting adolescence earlier than ever—some even by age eight!—and staying in it longer. We hope this manual will leave you feeling prepared and able to enjoy this astonishing transformative process. (Of course this book is only a general guide, and there is no substitute for discussing individual questions and concerns about your teenager with a healthcare provider.) At the end of this process your son or daughter will be plunging into the big world, ready to make a difference (in a good way, of course). Ideally, your child will be on a unique path of exploration, prepared to meet the challenges, perils, and joys of life with resiliency, humor, and curiosity. And a call home to the parents every once in awhile would be nice, too.

Congratulations, and welcome to the world of parenting a teen!

This manual has been shaped by the wisdom and expertise of the highly esteemed, board-certified adolescent medicine specialist Dr. Janice Hillman. Dr. Hillman, whose two daughters have already completed the teenage experience, has been practicing for more than twenty years in the University of Pennsylvania Health System. She contributes the "Doc Talk" sidebars that appear throughout the chapters that follow.

TEENAGE CLASS SYSTEM: Unfortunately, teenage friendships and

OUTSIDER

NERD

POPULAR

BULLY

cial standings are largely affected by labels.

Teens often gravitate to different social groups depending on their personality,

METALHEAD

ANGSTY REBEL

WALLFLOWER

PREPPY

ppearance, and hobbies or interests. Where does your teen fit in?

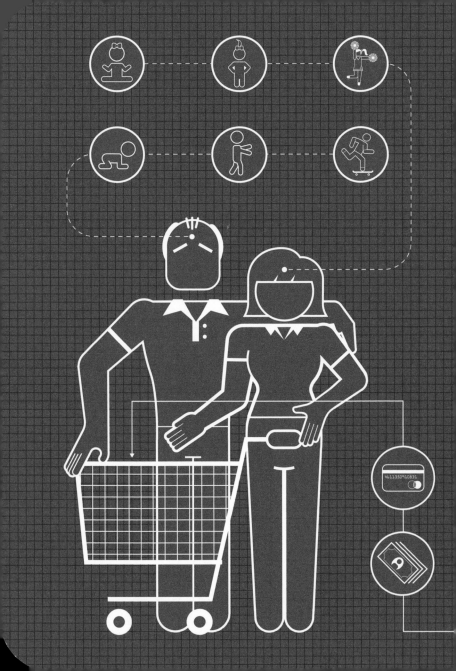

Chapter 1

Cram Session:

Prepping for the Teen Years

Maybe it was that day recently when your daughter had a serious mood swing: happily talking about the school dance one moment and then becoming distraught over who she would go with the next. You stopped what you were doing, your ears pricked up suddenly, your eyes darted over to the gangly child before you, and you sniffed the air warily. Yes, there was change in the air, and it smelled like teen spirit. You and your child had somehow arrived at the threshold of the teen years.

Brave New World:
Understanding What's Motivating Your Teen

For most parents, once we know what to expect and what to do, life seems more manageable. This applies to getting through the teen years as well. Some parents have horrendous experiences with wildly rebellious and infuriating children. But most parents experience something less dramatic yet still unfamiliar. In either case, the more parents know what is "driving" their teen, the more equipped they will be to react appropriately and to keep the arguments and clamor of everyday teen living to a minimum. This is just another one of those developmental stages to get through. It's not forever. (Though, depending on how many children you have, you may be stuck reliving adolescence a few more times.)

First, let's list your teen's developmental tasks. These are biologically driven goals that all teens accomplish, whether they are conscious of them or not:

■ To understand and become confident in that growing adolescent body. (Your kid will learn how to feed, operate, and maintain her new body.)

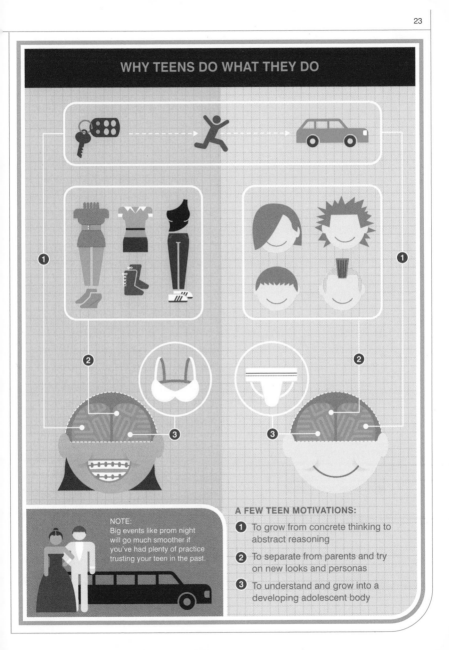

- To grow from concrete thinking to abstract, nuanced reasoning. (Finally, your teen can convincingly explain to you why he needs to take your car on a road trip with his buddies to hear their favorite band.)
- To separate from parents and try on new personas, yet be comforted by parents' unconditional love. (No matter how outrageous his rockstar-wannabe haircut is, he knows you're good for a hug.)
- To have control over choices and decisions (even when it makes Dad gnash his teeth to see his daughter date the homeroom lothario).
- To "individuate"—that is, establish autonomy and a distinctly separate personality and point of view from the parents'—and to rely on an inner voice for guidance. (No one wants Mom showing up at college to pick out majors or friends.)

These tasks are worthy goals for someone who has a relatively brief amount of time to gain self-mastery before going off to college or some other life beyond the family nest. But they often put the teen and parent in conflict. Strife flares because your teen thinks she's ready for more than you are willing to concede. Drive overnight with friends to catch the latest Radiohead concert? No way, you think. But your challenge is to let go a little and provide opportunities for growth that are safe and appropriate for your teen's evolving maturity level. You need to practice trusting your teen: in other words, lots of baby steps before that senior prom overnight bash.

By parenting with respect and attention, you can build your child's "résumé" of experiences:

- He'll learn how the world works by experiencing successes or, even more valuable, failures. There's nothing like a hangover headache and bout of volcanic vomiting to teach him to steer clear of Jagermeister—forever.

■ Your active parenting, with thoughtful limit-setting tied to predictable and reasonable consequences, will help him build his self-confidence to learn how to take good care of himself. He'll soon learn that "everyone's doing it" is not a sufficient reason to spend an entire weekend playing Guitar Hero.

The Most Important Habits of a Highly Successful Parent

Your teen needs a lot of your time because he will be working hard to figure out how to live in a complex social world. It's confusing, and kids need help. They don't want you to solve their problems for them or to meddle, but they do want you to support them as they solve their own problems.

Give Me Your Unconditional Love

Parents are usually not shocked by the type of teen their child turns into. Unruly tots can become challenging teens, and placid kids are often easygoing teens. But regardless of temperament and teen style, all children need to feel the security and warmth of their parents' unconditional love. It's not all they need, but it's something they definitely need.

It's nice to know that when we go out into the world and make an idiot of ourselves, we can always retreat and recover at home. Kids need to feel that way, too. Show them you love them, especially when their behavior is terrible. That's when they're feeling the most vulnerable.

Give Me Your Unconditional Love, Part 2

Your teen reserves for you the special role of witness to her worst behavior. You are a safe place to dump her least adorable impulses. Remember that hissy fit at the mall when you wouldn't buy her the ridiculously expensive designer jeans? Or the explosive response when you asked him to take out the recycling bins?

Believe it or not, your child is experiencing normal anxiety about separating from you, which perversely takes the form of unattractive behavior directed precisely at the person she most worries about being distanced from. Illogical? Yes. Uncommon? No. Despite being on the receiving end of flare-ups, back-talk, and mercurial whim:

■ Recognize it for what it is, and refrain from lashing out in outrage or hurt feelings.
■ Present a tight smile, and bite your tongue.
■ Address the issue of back-talk or general sassiness at a later time, when you can reason with your teen and your blood pressure has lowered.

⊞ *DOC TALK: Parents always ask me why they have to be the mature ones and reason with their child's irrational behavior. It's because you're the parent and it's your job to keep trying. You must set the example, and you must continue to teach. You must be the first to embrace the critical adage "life is not fair" if you want your children to cope with the unfairness of life situations.*

Amp Up Your Child's Inner Voice

Do you remember that kid on the playground who seemed to have absolutely nothing keeping him from obvious danger? He was the one running up to the big kids and trying to join in their roughhousing, or flinging himself off the highest part of the climber, or taunting a lost dog with a stick. You looked at this child and wondered, "How will he ever survive past snack time?"

Some kids have a very loud inner voice that guides them to safety and away from danger, whereas others seem to have absolutely none—or a very quiet one. But every child's innate judgment can be strengthened with practice, starting at an early age. Their common sense, ideally, guides them to more positive outcomes.

■ Say your young teen finds herself at a friend's party where kids from a neighboring school arrive with drugs, kids are pairing off for sexual encounters, and no adult is within a hundred-foot radius. Will her self-preservation impulses start broadcasting with urgency: "SOS! Call Mom and get me out of here!"?

■ Or say your child's peers are encouraging her to try dangerous behaviors. Will they be drowned out by her own voice and confident assessment that she is not in a smart place and needs to leave?

These assessments are a lot harder for teens whose parents order them around. Rigid, authoritarian parenting makes children receptive to peer pressure and taking orders from others. They have not practiced and flexed those muscles of thinking for themselves. This common-sense inner voice is a critical component if your teen is going to be successful navigating new situations that will test his mettle. (Cheat on a test? Shoplift at the mall? Pop some pills with friends to cram for an important test? No, thanks.)

[1] One of the easiest ways a parent can develop a child's inner voice and common sense is to give him choices to make. If there are two ways home from school, let your kid pick the way home. At the sneaker store, give him a price range and let him choose the shoe. Start when the stakes are not high and you are comfortable with either choice. Nike Dunks or checkerboard Vans? Your call, champ.

[2] Develop your child's flexible thinking and "shades of gray" reasoning by talking over what you see in your daily lives or on television:

- Ask your child whether she thought some action she witnessed was right.
- Ask her what she thinks the person should have done.
- Ask her whether the person could have made a better choice.

The world is bursting with teachable moments that can be drawn from playground politics, radio reports, articles in the newspaper, the lyrics to a song, and even snippets of conversation overheard at the supermarket. If you want a courageous, independent thinker, get your teen in the habit of challenging groupthink. (That is, when you are not commanding her to do her homework.)

⊕ *DOC TALK: I teach teens to recognize those gut feelings of "Hmm, this does not seem smart" and "I am really not sure if I should . . ." Those ambivalent feelings are a child's conscience telling him or her to stop, get away, or say no. Teens need to learn to trust those feelings!*

Develop the Problem-Solving Mind

If your teen presents you with a problem, you may be tempted simply to tell him what you'd do in the same situation. But this does not give him the practice he needs to put on his own problem-solving hat.

[1] Ask him to describe the problem and then talk through the various ways to proceed so he can be less black-and-white about his choices.

[2] Have him play through the consequences of each course of action. Ask him to describe both the immediate and long-term results.

[3] Be a problem-solving coach. Listening to him repeat "I'm doomed" isn't going to get that term paper written. But talking about problem-solving a lot will train your child not to go to that unproductive, passive despair mode. It is a powerful message that problems can be fixed with action. Encourage him to break the task into bite-sized pieces. (Remember that rallying cry from Bob the Builder? "Can we fix it? Yes we can!!")

Sometimes teens don't even realize how surmountable a problem really is. If your daughter is moaning about not being included in a certain circle of friends, ask if there are ways she could think of joining them. She might say, "Well, they all go out for pizza on Fridays in a neighborhood across town." Ask if you can drive her there. Voilà!

When a teen struggles with a tough situation, however, remember to recognize and praise the process she uses to come to grips with it. Compliment the skills she uses, not the end result. She still may not get invited to the party she wants to attend, but at least she had the courage to try.

Children also learn a lot by watching you problem-solve:

■ If your family's flight is canceled, instead of stomping around, go to the information desk and ask about alternate flights, or consider renting a car or grabbing a meal until new information is available.

■ Talk out loud as you sift and consider your choices. Let your teen hear your decision-making process and watch you stay calm.

It is good for everyone to find a way to fix a problem without anyone losing their composure.

Listen!

Teens like to be able to ask their parents about anything. They may not always take advantage of your open lines of communication, but it's nice for them to know they're there when they need them. Just keep repeating, "You can ask me about anything." One day you may be surprised to hear your teen opening up about something quite serious. He may casually drop a question about a "friend" who is being bullied or a kid at school who has an STD or someone's parent who died of lung cancer from smoking.

[1] When your teen does talk to you, keep yourself from interrupting. It can be hard to do, but it's worth it to clam up and just listen.

[2] Don't simply listen for a pause so you can jump in with your lecture. Listen respectfully and with an open mind. Keep any judgments to yourself.

[3] Try not to look so tickled and excited that he's opening up to you. You don't want to startle him back into a wary retreat and into his room.

Start the Conversation

A lot of teens tend to isolate themselves with friends or their computers instead of taking time to speak with parents. Let's face it: YouTube can be a lot more entertaining than a heart-to-heart with Dad. Build some family rituals into your home life to guarantee opportunities to talk.

■ Have meals together as much as possible. Aim for at least three or four times a week, if not more. Mealtime is a great time for kids to talk about their day and discuss issues on their minds. It creates a closeness that naturally leads to sharing.

■ If regular meals are difficult to maintain, try for a shared snack time or Sunday brunch. Chowing down on a plate of nachos could open up a conversation on sharing, fairness, and greed. Teens have a lot of opinions on what's fair. Sneak some more chips on your plate while they're busy talking.

■ When you do sit down together, remember to turn off the television or radio so there are no distractions. Make it a rule to ignore phone calls until after the meal.

■ Don't allow your kids to use handheld electronics or iPods when you are all together as a family. It's easy for a child to retreat into his own world if he's zoning out to his latest download.

■ Keep the home computer in a public space. If your teen is on the computer in the family room, you'll be able to tell when he's been on way too long. Computers, Internet, and e-mail can gobble up huge chunks of time, and screen time limits face-time between you and your child.

■ Schedule a walk or other activity (going out for a snack, or a drive to the hardware store). You don't have to go with the intention of having a heavy talk, but eventually conversation will happen naturally when you are striding along side by side. Sometimes becoming absorbed in an activity can loosen lips. Boys, in particular, get chattier when they are busy doing something.

■ Most important, let your child know just how much you love (and like) him. If your teen knows you value him and enjoy his company, he's more likely to value himself, and a sense of self-worth is invaluable when it comes to fending off nasty peer pressure.

EXPERT TIP: *If your teen has learning issues or a chronic physical illness, be wary of connecting with her exclusively on matters surrounding her special needs. If all you do is harass your daughter about finishing her homework or talk about academic challenges, your conversations will become negatively charged. Put special effort into dropping the hot-potato topics and talk about something completely different.*

Don't Rule with an Iron Fist

Controlling your teen is a failing proposition. Simply put, it never works! Of course this does not mean you have to live in anarchy. Enforceable and clear house and family rules are required for everyone's sense of security and peace of mind. If tacky, rude T-shirts offend you, for example, make a "no tacky T-shirt" rule.

But enforcement of rules is another thing entirely. As a parent, you can no longer physically extract your son from a struggle with his brother over Legos and put him in the time-out chair.

[1] Clearly lay out a few simple house rules and the consequences that will follow if they're broken.

[2] Don't forget to explain the reason behind the rules.

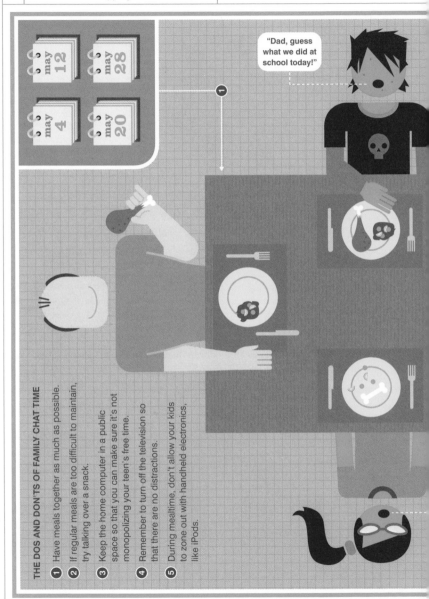

THE DOS AND DON'TS OF FAMILY CHAT TIME

1. Have meals together as much as possible.

2. If regular meals are too difficult to maintain, try talking over a snack.

3. Keep the home computer in a public space so that you can make sure it's not monopolizing your teen's free time.

4. Remember to turn off the television so that there are no distractions.

5. During mealtime, don't allow your kids to zone out with handheld electronics, like iPods.

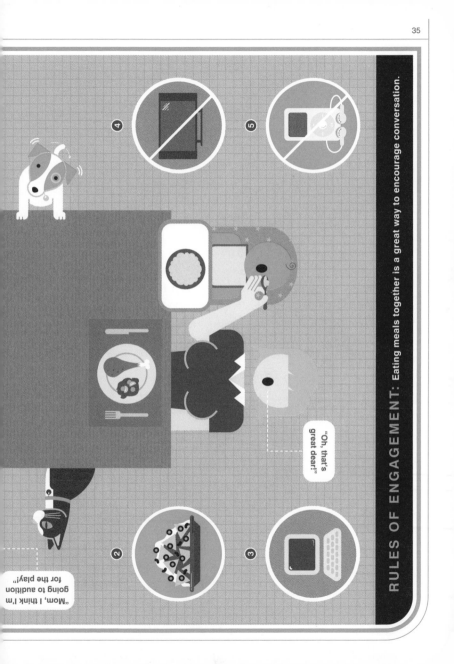

RULES OF ENGAGEMENT: Eating meals together is a great way to encourage conversation.

[3] If a rule is broken, be sure to find out why. Talk it over and get your child's explanation. She may surprise you with her point of view.

[4] Follow up with whatever consequences or loss of privileges has been outlined. You don't want to be thought of as a wimp.

How to Be a Super Model

Parents are very powerful role models. What children see you do will define the boundaries of appropriate behavior for them: If you are snappish at your spouse, your child will internalize this as okay behavior. Parents who do a lot of hollering will raise kids who do a lot of hollering right back. Kids have an uncanny way of absorbing family values just by witnessing them day after day. So:

■ If you don't want your son to swear like a sailor, don't use profanity.

■ If you don't want your daughter to let her frustration get the best of her, don't give in to frustration the next time you're stuck in traffic while driving her to school.

■ If you don't want your teen to abuse alcohol, then don't have an after-work cocktail every day or get tipsy in front of him.

Let you child see you experience genuine remorse or change your mind. If you make mistakes, acknowledge them, and go on with your life. It's inspiring for your teen to see that you can laugh at your own mistakes and try to do better next time. She certainly knows you're not perfect, but what she's now seeing is how adults live with imperfections and still retain their self-esteem. Remember this when you are struggling to parallel park in front of the local movie theater to drop off your

teen. As your kid's friends start to snicker, laugh it off and tell your child that practice makes perfect.

Parents who take care of themselves and who take pleasure in the companionship of their marriage also set wonderful examples for their teens. If your teen sees you eating healthfully, exercising, socializing with friends, getting enough sleep, taking pleasure in learning new things, being respectful toward others, and enjoying life, you will be shaping your child's expectations of what he or she aspires to as an adult.

You Are Not Your Child

Be prepared for self-discovery as you suffer through your child's coming-of-age moments. Be aware: Pretty much all parents unwittingly relive their own teen years and churn through a lot of ancient history during their kids' adolescence.

You'll need to prepare yourself emotionally, because your beliefs and values will all be called into question by your child. And it can be hugely unsettling to realize your own hard-won beliefs might be in need of some updating and modifications.

Questioning your own hang-ups might reveal insecurities. Freaked out about whether your teen is popular? How your teen looks? Whether his clothes are dorky? Your teen's success as an athlete? How your child is a reflection of you? Enmeshment and over-identification with your child can muddy the waters when it comes to parenting. Ask yourself: Are you merely reacting to the situation at hand, or are you dragging along emotional baggage you've been carrying since your own teen years? Try as much as you can to separate your teen experience from your child's, and you'll be on much firmer ground. Just because you had bad eighties hair as a teen doesn't mean your kids will suffer the same hair angst. Just because they didn't make the sports team doesn't mean they're crushed, like you were.

⚕ *DOC TALK: In my experience, the parents who struggle and fight the most with their teens are the parents who have the most internal struggle with who they are themselves. I often recommend therapy for the parents along with therapy for the teen when a family is having difficulties. Communication improves when both parties are in tune with their motivations and feelings.*

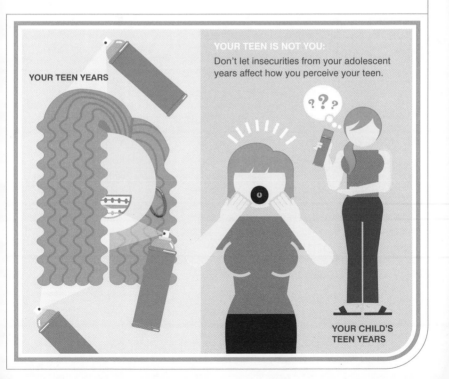

Chapter 2

Physical Education:

The Changing Body and Mind of Your Teen

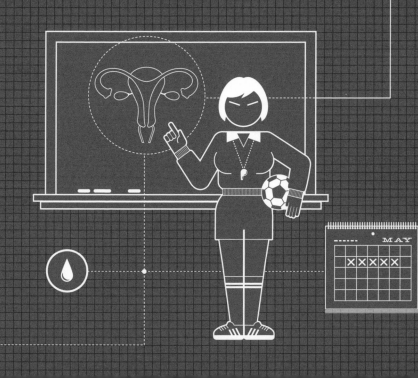

All a teen really wants to be is "normal" and blend in. God forbid any teen should attract attention. Teenagers tend to be excruciatingly self-conscious, so to be the first to get pubic hair? No thank you. The girl with the biggest breasts? Not on your life. The boy who keeps getting spontaneous erections in English class? No way.

Most kids want to run with the pack when it comes to puberty—neither out in front nor left behind. But normal development unfolds on such a broad spectrum that many kids can feel shaky about where they stand. Your job as a parent is to answer questions and offer reassurance along the way.

You can imagine how confused and saucer-eyed a boy could feel about his first "wet dream" or a girl's anxiety when she experiences her first menstrual period without any preparation. As a parent, you need to proactively tell your son or daughter what changes to expect—both physically and emotionally. Not only will having the right information bolster your teen's confidence, but it will protect him or her from believing urban legends or wacky facts passed on by other confused kids. ("Ryan told me you can tell if someone masturbates because the palms of their hands are hairy. Or was it they get acne? Or go bald? Um . . .")

It's All in the Timing:
His and Her Puberty

Every individual body runs on its own particular timetable, but the end of elementary school and most of middle school is typically considered the Hot Zone of human adolescent development.

■ The brain and certain glands get the process in motion by increasing the production of hormones. (The sex hormones are the same in both boys and girls, and both estrogen and testosterone are present in both sexes. What differs is the amount and the degree to which the body responds to the hormone.)

■ The hormones begin to create striking physical changes, and also do a number on your teen's emotional equilibrium. This is normal, folks!

■ Girls tend to enter puberty about two years before boys do, at around age 10 or 11, but it can happen anytime between ages 9 and 13 as well.

■ Boys typically begin puberty around age 12, but it can also happen anytime between ages 11 and 14.

EXPERT TIP: *Sometimes a child will experience puberty at an extremely early age, in a condition known as "precocious puberty." If a daughter starts puberty before age 8 or a son before age 9, you should contact the child's doctor to make sure no underlying medical conditions are involved.*

I Smell a Teenager

The start of puberty can be subtle. Depending on your child's modesty, you might even totally miss the first signs (a daughter's development of breast buds and pubic hair or a son's testicular development). Your child could be a full year into puberty before you notice, but usually your first clue will be a whiff of body odor. As apocrine glands begin to produce more sweat, the sweat mixes with bacteria and causes smells from the armpits or crotch.

There are a few factors that can predict when puberty will start, though nothing is a sure bet.

Family history. The age at which the mom or dad began puberty often predicts when the same-sex child will begin. If a mom wonders when her daughter will begin menstruating, she could make a good guess by recalling her own age when menses began.

Weight. Obesity or extra pounds can trigger the process. A child's excess body fat can signal the brain to begin maturation early. Conversely, underweight children tend to experience delayed puberty. Girl athletes with particularly low body fat might have delayed menstruation (called primary amenorrhea) or may stop menstruating once they've experienced their first episode (called secondary amenorrhea).

The speed with which a child moves through puberty also varies. Some go through the entire process in one year; others take as long as six years. The average, however, is three to four years from start to finish.

⚠ **EXPERT TIP:** *An adolescent's body might begin the process, then slow down or stop before starting up and moving forward again. Even when all the secondary sexual characteristics are in place, a boy or girl can continue growing. Some do not finish until their late teens.*

Early and Later Signs of Puberty for Girls

The earliest indications that your daughter is beginning to move into puberty include:

■ Breast buds. These buds are small bumps that grow underneath the nipple. The breast buds can be mildly sensitive to touch and may also be asymmetric in size. (Boys will sometimes develop small buds because their hormone production has increased. Not to worry. This condition, called gynecomastia, usually resolves within eighteen months.)

■ Hair growth in armpits and pubic area.

■ Body odor.

As your daughter's body continues to mature, you'll notice these later signs as well:

■ Her breasts grow in size and shape; the vagina creates discharge; and the uterus, ovaries, and fallopian tubes grow.

■ Menstruation occurs. A girl's first period usually follows about one to two years after the onset of puberty. The average age is 12 for a first menstrual period, but anytime between the ages of 9 and 15 is considered normal. (Outside of those ranges a doctor should be consulted.)

■ Her pubic hair coarsens and fills in.

■ She experiences a growth spurt, usually one to two years after the onset of puberty. Girls are often finished growing before boys begin. Girls tend to lengthen and strengthen bones first, then add muscle mass, then fat. Weight gain occurs in hips and thighs. She's got curves!

■ She begins to have oilier skin, and, for some girls, alas, acne.

⊞ *DOC TALK: I get many calls from moms about vaginal discharge. It is completely normal and healthy that, as a girl's vagina matures, it produces a clear or white mucous. If the discharge is colored, smelly, or itchy, speak with your healthcare provider. Some girls might want to wear a panty liner for comfort.*

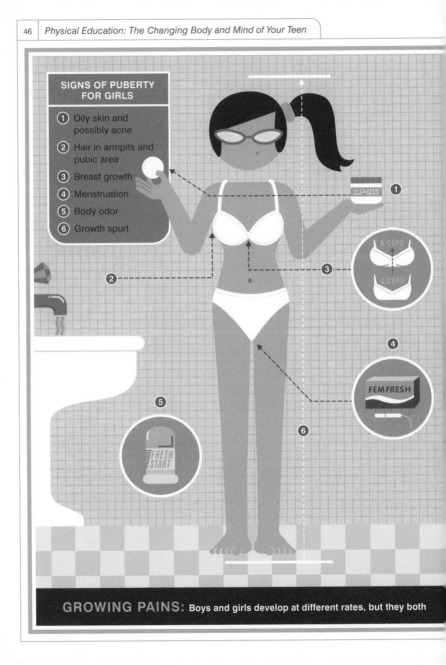

SIGNS OF PUBERTY FOR GIRLS

1. Oily skin and possibly acne
2. Hair in armpits and pubic area
3. Breast growth
4. Menstruation
5. Body odor
6. Growth spurt

GROWING PAINS: Boys and girls develop at different rates, but they both

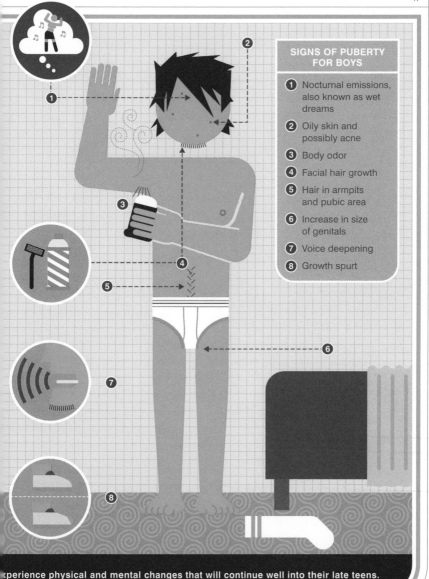

SIGNS OF PUBERTY FOR BOYS

1. Nocturnal emissions, also known as wet dreams
2. Oily skin and possibly acne
3. Body odor
4. Facial hair growth
5. Hair in armpits and pubic area
6. Increase in size of genitals
7. Voice deepening
8. Growth spurt

...xperience physical and mental changes that will continue well into their late teens.

Early and Later Signs of Puberty for Boys

The earliest indications that your son is beginning to begin the maturation process and move into puberty include:

- Increase in size of testicles.
- Hair growth in armpits and pubic area.
- Nocturnal emissions, also know as "wet dreams."
- Body odor.

As your son's body continues to mature, you'll notice these later signs as well:

- His penis lengthens and thickens; the scrotum darkens and hangs lower.
- His pubic hair coarsens and fills in.
- His facial hair grows.
- His voice box (the larynx) grows, as do his vocal cords, which deepen his voice.
- He experiences a growth spurt. His feet and hands typically grow first, then his legs and arms, and finally the trunk of his body. Boys tend to grow bones and muscle proportionately. They can grow 4 to 6 inches in height in one year, though the entire growth period can last for two or three years. No wonder some kids complain of growing pains!
- He begins to have oilier skin, and, for some boys, acne.

All About Breasts

Most girls greet signs of their breast development with a combination of awe, pride, and embarrassment. The good news is that there are not many "maintenance" issues to be concerned about when it comes to breasts. All they need is a good bra.

First, some breast facts:

[1] Breast growth begins with the arrival of breast buds. Hormones trigger the growth of breast tissue, fat, and glands under the nipple.

[2] The breasts continue to grow, often through a pointy stage, before arriving at the final adult-looking breast shape. The in-between phase is a tough one for many teen girls. They are too small for a bra but developed enough that their new silhouette makes them self-conscious. Some girls will double-up on tank tops or use training bras until they are ready for their first bra.

[3] Sometimes, breasts can develop at an uneven pace, with the results appearing a little or a lot lopsided. This will typically be resolved by the time they have reached the final stage of breast development, though not always.

[4] There is no such thing as a typical breast. Breasts come in many shapes and sizes, from barely there to large enough to cause back troubles.

[5] Breast size tends to run in the family. Heavy-breasted and small-breasted women often will have similarly sized daughters.

Many girls can't wait to wear their first bra, though some may feel ambivalent about no longer being a child. They might be reluctant to go bra shopping, even though they appear to be ready physically. As a parent, you might also be too busy or distracted to notice your daughter's growing need for breast support, especially if she's sporting big sweatshirts or bulky clothing. In any case, when you do both finally arrive at the moment to go bra shopping, there are some easy tips to keep in mind to minimize your daughter's possible mortification.

Embarrassment-Free Bra Shopping

Remember: Many teens are hyper self-conscious, and buying a bra for the first time might top a girl's list of emotionally loaded awkward experiences:

■ Consider inviting your daughter's close friend or big sister along for moral support. Definitely leave her little brother behind.

■ Bear in mind that your daughter may want to treat her bra-shopping expedition like a stealth undercover operation. She'll want the chance to call off the mission immediately if she sees any familiar faces. God forbid any boys from her school are sighted in the bra-shopping zone!

■ If your teen wants a bra but does not yet fill out a cup size, a sports bra is a good option. This will legitimately usher her into the bra-wearing club, and can smooth out some of the pointiness.

■ Consider bra shopping online or by catalog. This will allow you and your daughter to pore over options and study various features before making selections. You can order a few different sizes and styles and simply return the rejects. Sometimes this prospect is less overwhelming for a teen, and certainly spares her the embarrassment of running into her crush at the mall while lugging a shopping bag full of bras. Perhaps the biggest bonus is that

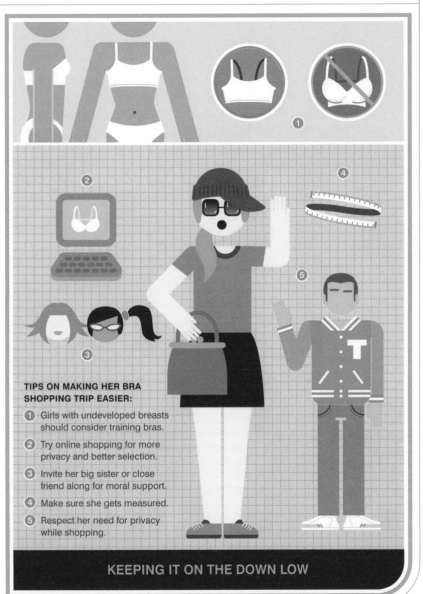

TIPS ON MAKING HER BRA SHOPPING TRIP EASIER:

1. Girls with undeveloped breasts should consider training bras.
2. Try online shopping for more privacy and better selection.
3. Invite her big sister or close friend along for moral support.
4. Make sure she gets measured.
5. Respect her need for privacy while shopping.

KEEPING IT ON THE DOWN LOW

your daughter can try on the bras at home, without the fear of a sales lady flinging the curtain open and asking if she needs help.

■ Be sure your daughter is measured for a proper fit. Many adult women end up wearing the wrong bra size simply because they have not been fitted properly. Measure carefully (see below) or go to a specialty store where she can be fitted by a professional. Your daughter should be remeasured every so often, too, since her breasts will continue to change until she completes the final stage of breast growth.

Getting the Right Bra Fit

Choosing the right bra size is tricky even for veteran shoppers who have been wearing bras for decades. The most common mistake is wearing a band—also called a "back"—size that is too large. Note, too, that bra sizes are not uniform across manufacturers, so just because your daughter has figured out she wears a 32B in one brand does not mean she will wear the same size in another. Remind her that a well-fitting bra should be comfortable but snug.

There are two ways to determine proper bra size. The first method is to get out a tape measure:

[1] Measure the width around the rib cage, directly under the breasts. If you get an odd number, round up to the next even one. This will give you the band size. The old-school method of adding four to five inches to the first measurement is likely the reason why so many women are wearing the wrong size. Don't fall into that trap!

[2] Measure the bust at its fullest part. If this measurement has a one-inch difference from the band size, your daughter's cup size is A. If there is a two-

inch difference, her cup size is B; for a three-inch difference, the cup is C; and for a four-inch difference, the cup is D.

[3] Keep in mind that cup sizes are proportional, too. A cup size D on a 30-inch band is smaller than a cup size D on a 38-inch band. If your daughter is trying on a bra that seems too big at a 36B, have her try a 34C.

The second method is to eyeball whatever bra your daughter tries on first, making size adjustments accordingly until your daughter gets the right fit.

[1] Look at the back of the bra. If it is on the tightest hooks, this may be a sign the band is too large. If you can pull the band backward and away from the body, it may also suggest the band is too large. If your daughter is wearing a 36B, get her a 34B and a 34C and have her determine the best fit.

[2] Check for strap marks on the shoulder area. If the straps are digging into the skin, the band may be too loose, forcing the straps to do the heavy lifting. Have your daughter try a smaller band. The straps may also simply be too tight.

[3] Check the view from the side. If the bra is not horizontal and it is tipping forward, the band may be too big and the bra too saggy. Again, have her try a smaller band.

[4] Check the cups. If breasts are popping over the front, the cup size is too small; have your daughter try a bigger cup size. If you can see dimpling and caved-in spots on the cup, have her try a smaller cup size. If the middle point of the bra is not flush against the breast bone, have her try a bigger cup size that encases the breast completely.

Know Your Bra-Buying Lingo

T-shirt bra: This bra is a teen essential. It's a regular bra without seams, so that when she wears a clingy T-shirt no bumps, ridges, or lines show through.

Underwire bra: These bras have wire or plastic lining the bottom of the cup for extra support. Underwire bras are designed for larger-breasted girls.

Padded bra: The cushioning built into this bra will make your teen's breasts seem larger. The padded bra is different from a push-up bra, which has a low-cut cup and padding below to push up the breasts for a more revealing look. Most parents will want to steer clear of the sexy push-up.

Sports bra: Essential for sports and also a good option for smaller-breasted girls.

Demi-cup bra: This is a low-cut, half-cup bra for low-cut clothing.

Strapless bra: The perfect solution for her strapless prom gown.

Minimizer bra: These bras compress the breasts to make them look as much as one cup size smaller. Most start at a C cup.

Menstrual Periods and Sympathy

Most teen girls get a pretty good sense of what menstrual periods are about by overhearing big sisters and neighborhood kids talk about them, or even from those fifth-grade health class discussions, when the boys are shepherded into one room and the girls to another. Your daughter may see commercials on television, come across print ads in magazines, or hear older girls talking on the bus about having their periods. But she still needs a positive and thorough discussion of the topic from you before she experiences her own first period.

Aim to have "the talk" when your daughter is around 10 years old. You'll be expanding on the more-encompassing "birds and bees" talk you've already delivered (see Chapter 4, page 147). Be sure to have some props on hand: Pads of various sorts, panty liners, and tampons will help familiarize your daughter with the important details.

It's Not a Curse!

Your daughter's first period is a momentous milestone, so be sure that she gets the message that her maturing body is a good thing and not something that should be ignored or joked about. Telling her that she will experience a "lifetime of hell" or that periods are "a curse" will only set her up for negative feelings about her body.

Take the time to review some of the basic facts, so she can gain an understanding of just what her body is doing and why:

[1] As her sexual organs mature, eggs ripen inside follicles located in the ovaries. Around midcycle, the egg will ovulate and break out of the ovary, traveling into the fallopian tube and toward the uterus.

[2] During ovulation, she may notice a thin, whitish vaginal discharge. This cervical fluid is intended to make it easier for sperm to swim upstream through the vagina.

[3] When the egg goes unfertilized, the uterus sheds its lining through the menstrual process, bleeding away the unused lining.

[4] Assure your daughter that menstrual blood won't just gush out without any warning! Your teen will initially notice a brownish tint when she wipes with toilet paper as well as a distinctive odor to the discharge. Be sure to explain these points to her, since this concept is usually one girls feel anxious about.

[5] As her body gets into full swing and sheds the uterine lining, the flow can be a deep red and may sometimes be filled with clotty tissue.

[6] As the period winds down, the flow will lighten, and the blood may look brownish once more.

[7] A menstrual period can typically last between three to seven days. Initially, most girls experience irregular menstrual cycles until their body matures into a predictable rhythm, although some immediately get into a monthly routine. The range between cycles, at that point, can be anywhere between 21 to 45 days. Encourage your daughter to keep a calendar so she can predict when she is due to get her next period.

PREPARATION IS HER BEST DEFENSE

TIPS TO HELP HER GET THROUGH HER FIRST PERIOD:

1. Store an extra set of clothing in locker.

2. Have her keep a tampon or pad and change for a tampon dispenser in her school bag.

3. In a pinch, she can use toilet paper as a makeshift feminine napkin.

4. Ask the school nurse for help.

Emergency Prep for Red-Letter Days

A lot of teen girls project worst-case scenarios about their first menstrual period: "I just know I'll get it when I'm wearing my white shorts, and I'll be at school, and no one will tell me, and it will be horrible . . ." Help your daughter strategize situations beforehand so that she can be prepared with an action plan:

■ Tell her to keep a pad, change of underwear, and even an extra pair of pants in her school locker. She can also keep an old sweater or hoodie in her locker. If need be, she can tie one around her waist until she can address the situation properly.

■ Tell her to keep a tampon or pad in her schoolbag or purse. Be sure she has coins with her in case she needs to use a public-bathroom tampon dispenser.

■ Tell her she can always wad up some toilet paper or tissue and use that as a makeshift pad until she can get the items she needs.

■ Talk to her about people she can turn to for help. Could she go to the school nurse or a female teacher or coach with whom she feels comfortable? Does she have an older sister or female friend who would know what to do?

Your daughter's first period signals that she's reached a significant milestone on her way to adulthood. She is fertile now, and she also now has to be responsible enough to manage the hygiene aspects of menstrual flow. Not changing a pad or tampon when it's due is a whole lot different from spacing out on your homework.

Explain the differences among pads and tampons to your daughter, and do your best to "demystify" how it all works. The variety and choices of products can be pretty baffling, but once she hits on the right one for her, she will find it all quite easy to manage. Be sure to debunk any sort of apprehensions about tampons (no, they can't get lost and travel into the body). Unwrapping one to show her the basic concept will help.

⊕ *DOC TALK: Here are some additional reminders regarding hygiene and menstruation that many parents find useful:*

■ *I still occasionally have moms who worry that tampons are not for virgins. Rest assured: The hymen, the thin membrane over the vagina, is almost always open by the time menses start.*

■ *Be sure to tell your daughter to steer clear of scented tampons that can irritate the vagina.*

■ *Similarly, feminine deodorants and douches are unnecessary and can lead to infections. If your daughter bathes or showers regularly, she will remain fresh. (Douching may actually tamper with the vagina's self-cleaning system and disrupt the balance of bacteria, which may make your teen more vulnerable to sexually transmitted diseases and bacterial and yeast infections.)*

Cramp Busters

Cramps usually crop up only during the first day or two of a menstrual period. All the same, let your daughter in on a few key strategies for dealing with them.

[1] She can start taking anti-inflammatory medication two to three days before her period starts. This helps block the prostaglandin enzyme that starts the cramps. Be sure to check with her health-care provider about the proper dose.

[2] Encourage her to empty her bladder often during her period. A full bladder can sometimes worsen cramps by pressing on the uterus.

[3] Introduce her to the benefits of an old-fashioned heating pad. Heating patches or pads transmit heat to the abdomen and thighs to alleviate cramping. Another DIY treatment favored by doulas to aid women in labor: Take a long gym sock, fill it with rice, and pop it into the microwave. Apply the heated sock to the area where trouble is lurking to relax those tight muscles.

[4] Encourage her to eat a light diet during her period.

[5] Encourage her to exercise. Physical exertion can release painkilling endorphins that will short-circuit cramps. It may also simply distract her from her cramping muscles. Yoga poses, especially Child's Pose and the cat and dog postures, are also excellent ways to combat cramping.

Rogue Penises:
What's Going on Down There?

Certain aspects of your son's passage through puberty may fly under the radar. Unlike his female counterpart, whose breasts start forming in early puberty, a boy's development can go undetected. He may also start to close the door a lot as he experiments with his changing body.

[1] Let him know that privacy is okay, but so is his changing body. Give him plenty of opportunities to ask you questions about anything and everything.

[2] Your son's genitalia will grow in measurable stages (his pediatrician will be taking note to see that he's progressing through puberty; see page 48). First the testicles grow, and then the penis. As puberty progresses, the scrotum's skin becomes thinner and hangs more. It will also darken in color.

[3] The penis will widen and lengthen as puberty continues. Pubic hair will be sparse at first and then coarsen and spread outward.

Nocturnal Emissions 101

You should not be surprised that your son is getting erections. He's actually been getting them—or has been capable of sprouting them—since he was a baby. The difference now is that he can ejaculate sperm. Once puberty arrives, his testicles are producing enough testosterone to make sperm, which is mixed with semen.

When do boys discover that they can make ejaculate? Usually the discovery is made in the privacy of their own room or bathroom during experimentation with masturbation or because of a nocturnal emission, more often referred to as a "wet dream." Wet dreams are often a source of mystery and embarrassment for boys.

■ A boy might wake up in the middle of the night or in the morning with sticky, damp pajamas. He might catch on quick what it is but not know why it's there. (Some boys may worry that they've peed in their bed unless a parent explains the difference.)

■ Wet dreams may make some kids feel anxious, especially if they have seen or heard about other boys having spontaneous erections in the middle of school. They already know that penises are highly reactive to thoughts, images, and even simple pressure or touch. Reassure your son that although spontaneous erections may happen during the day, they will not result in spontaneous ejaculation.

If you walk into your son's room in the morning and notice the sheets are wet, just hand the boy a towel. Act casual and say, "Eh, don't worry.

That's normal. Happens to all guys." He may be mortified that you have acknowledged his situation, but he will be relieved to hear it's natural, and that you're not fazed by it—even if you are. Save your astonishment for the privacy of the laundry room.

Spontaneous Erections and Other Surprises

Spontaneous erections are another source of worry for boys. Your son might be in the middle of a trombone lesson or science class and not doing anything the least bit arousing, when whammo: erect penis. If your teen has expressed this as a worry—the rogue penis doing its own thing—problem-solve some tactics he might use to go flaccid. And even if he doesn't tell you about his concerns, you should try to introduce the topic during a car ride or some other quiet moment.

If you're the dad, offer a childhood story from your past. You can add, "I was thinking, I was about your age when it first happened." If you're the mom, you might introduce the topic by relating stories your brothers or your spouse told you. Then offer some ideas about what he could do when he finds himself in a similar situation:

■ Tell him to think about the stock market. Or his grandparents. Or sports. Or a looming term paper. Something very un-sexy.

■ Teach him some cognitive distraction tricks: Have him think of state capitals; sing the national anthem to himself (if he can remember the words); or recite the presidents of the United States backward.

■ Recommend that he wear briefs or boxer-briefs to keep the action close to the body. Buy him some baggy pants for further camouflage.

■ Have him untuck his shirt and let it hang loose in front.

■ Instruct him to keep his books or book bag in front of his privates.

■ For very highly evolved and practical parents: Advise him to masturbate before school so that it reduces the chances of spontaneous erection during class time. Just be aware that if you offer this suggestion, you may cause him to go into a catatonic state of embarrassment.

Support the Team!

If your son plays a certain kind of sport (football, baseball, ice hockey, lacrosse, etc.), you will need to get him a good jockstrap that supports the genitals and a cup to protect the family jewels. You can find cups and jocks at sporting goods stores.

■ The protective cup will shield him from injury. It is inserted into the jockstrap to buffer against ferocious hockey sticks, lacrosse balls, cruel football tackles, and the like. (Make sure you buy the strap specifically designed to hold athletic cups.)
■ Cups come in a variety of sizes, so check to make sure it's the right size and provides full protective coverage.
■ The cup should have ventilation and a contoured shape for comfort.
■ The fit needs to be comfortable, but snug.

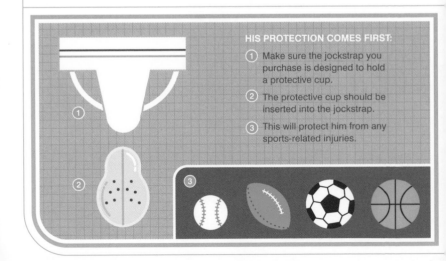

HIS PROTECTION COMES FIRST:
1. Make sure the jockstrap you purchase is designed to hold a protective cup.
2. The protective cup should be inserted into the jockstrap.
3. This will protect him from any sports-related injuries.

Masturbation Is Not a Dirty Word

If you were paying close enough attention as a new mother or father, you may have noticed a time when your infant was masturbating. Little kids, especially little boys, love to fiddle with their private parts. They are delighted to have a little penis to play with in the tub or while being changed. By a certain age, they learn to be a bit more discrete about their recreational pursuits.

It's Only Natural

Boys and girls need to know that masturbation is a normal and useful practice for developing a deeper appreciation of their sexuality and sexual responses. You can alleviate a lot of your child's anxiety by casually affirming that it's a natural function, that most people have masturbated at one time or another, and that some masturbate quite frequently.

If you find a stiff wash cloth or hand towel buried under your son's bed, you have likely come across a "masturbation rag." Or if you notice he's suddenly washing the sheets or comforter on his bed—a lot—chances are he's discovered self-pleasuring. Here's your chance to take advantage of the situation and ask him to move along the wash while he's hanging out in the laundry room.

[1] If you happen upon your son or daughter masturbating, treat the moment as you would if you walked in on them while undressing. Give your teen some privacy and holler a brief apology through the door.

[2] Later, if you are feeling crazily brave, mention that you noticed what was going on and reaffirm that masturbation is healthy.

[3] Ask your child if he wants to talk about it or if he has any questions. Your son's heart may stop beating temporarily at this "open line of communication," but it will establish your gutsy willingness to talk about anything.

EXPERT TIP: *The only caveat about masturbation is that it should not go overboard. It should not be used in place of developing a relationship with a person or other daily activities. Some boys are obsessed and go through a period when they might do it four or five times a day. Some will masturbate before a date to prevent against getting overly aroused and ejaculating prematurely. This might be a time to utter the refrain: Everything in moderation.*

You Really Won't Go Blind

Old wives' tales have long held the power to unnerve young boys and girls alike when it comes to masturbation. Give your kids the facts.

If your teen masturbates . . .

- he or she will not go insane.
- he or she will not go bald.
- he or she will not go blind.
- he or she will not grow hair on the palms.
- he will not run out of sperm.
- he or she will not get acne.
- his or her sexual orientation will not be affected.
- he or she will still be a virgin.

In fact, masturbation can . . .

- reduce stress.
- teach the teen about his or her body.
- possibly even reduce headaches and menstrual cramps.

Keeping It Clean with Teen Hygiene

What makes people smell bad? The short answer is bacteria. Perspiration in itself isn't smelly, but when it interacts with bacteria that live on skin, it can morph into a funk that could stop a truck—or at least cause your child's friends to take a seat at a different table in the lunchroom.

Our bodies have eccrine and apocrine sweat glands. It is the latter that populates more densely around three areas: armpits, nipples, and genitals. When bacteria feed off the proteins in apocrine sweat, it releases a strong stink. (Not so for eccrine-produced sweat.) That's why underarms and genital areas can become particularly pungent. In earlier times, this chemical signaling of our bodies was helpful in selecting the ideal mate, but today BO just won't fly with your home-room hottie.

Frequent showering and changing clothes will help eliminate sweat-loving bacteria. With fewer bacteria on the body, there's less smell. Most teens are acutely aware of their new odor and will monopolize the bathroom to combat this malodorous adolescent development.

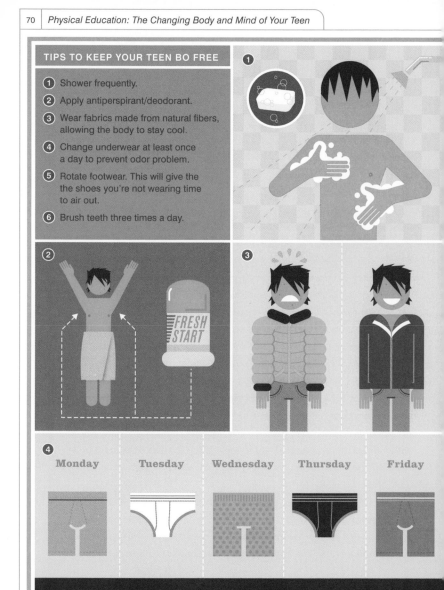

TIPS TO KEEP YOUR TEEN BO FREE

1. Shower frequently.
2. Apply antiperspirant/deodorant.
3. Wear fabrics made from natural fibers, allowing the body to stay cool.
4. Change underwear at least once a day to prevent odor problem.
5. Rotate footwear. This will give the the shoes you're not wearing time to air out.
6. Brush teeth three times a day.

FRESH START

Monday	Tuesday	Wednesday	Thursday	Friday

SMELLS LIKE TEEN SPIRIT: Now that your teen's body is developing,

Remember to brush the tongue too. Most odors originate from the back of the tongue, where bacterial plaque builds up.

weat glands are in full effect, which means that body odor is more common.

BO Be Gone!

Remember that cleanliness goes along with self-esteem. It shows that a kid respects himself enough to take care of his body.

Cleanliness may (or may not) be next to godliness, but it sure will help your teen get next to whomever he's flirting with in the school hallways. Here's what he can do:

- Shower frequently.
- Apply antiperspirant/deodorant daily.
- Wear fabrics made from natural fibers that breathe more easily, allowing the body to remain cool and not sweat. (Synthetic fabrics trap heat and raise body temperatures, causing sweat and, thus, odor.)
- Wear only freshly laundered clothes. Clothes that have been sweated on will cook up odors.
- Change underwear at least once a day—more frequently if there's a strong odor problem. Unclean underwear can be a real stench-producer.
- Give sneakers the day off to air out. Bacteria feed on moist conditions. Rotate sneakers so that the off-duty pair can dry out completely.
- Brush teeth at least three times a day, and remember to brush the tongue, too. Most odors originate from the back of the tongue, where bacterial plaque builds up.

Going Mental:
This Is Your Teen's Brain on Hormones

Teens try to persuade us they are ready for the adult world, but even the most "together" teen has not completed brain growth. Most kids' brains change considerably throughout adolescence—and even into their early twenties. (Important note: Because the brain is still developing, it is vulnerable, particularly to alcohol and drugs.)

So there are brain-based excuses for a teen's moodiness, inability to plan, and erratic reasoning. And there are also brain-based reasons for hope: Once that prefrontal cortex matures, you're golden! (Unfortunately, this is the last section of the brain to mature.)

The basic process of brain development goes like this:

[1] The brain overproduces brain cells and synapses in infancy that are reduced and "organized" around age 3.

[2] From age 3 to early adolescence, a child's gray matter thickens once more.

[3] Right before puberty, the child's brain experiences a brain growth spurt before the second major consolidation. This streamlining makes for more sophisticated and efficient brain function.

My Amygdala Made Me Do It!
Or, What's Really Happening to Your Child's Brain

Parents the world over observe similar patterns of spacy and impulsive behavior in their teens, but now there's solid research to back up what everyone's been witnessing all along. It may not help to know that your child's brain is undergoing massive change at this stage of life, but perhaps you'll have just a smidgen more sympathy for him when he starts acting particularly goofy.

[1] While your teenager's brain may be almost adult size by puberty, his brain's nerve connections are slow and comparatively inefficient. To help the brain accomplish activities with much greater speed and complexity, his nerve connections need to grow a sophisticated covering of material known as myelin. Teenage brains have limited myelin sheaths in early puberty that often don't mature completely until his early twenties.

[2] To top that off, your teen's myelin is also unevenly distributed throughout his brain. There is less myelin in his frontal lobes and more myelin in the part of his brain that's responsible for emotional reactions, known as the amygdala. When your teen is required to make a decision, his amygdala jumps to the task because it's more powerful than the frontal lobes.

[3] And what happens when your teen's amygdala makes a decision? Well, it's not for nothing that decisions from the amygdala are known as "gut reactions": They are emotional judgments that do not have the benefit of fully developed frontal lobes to do a safety inspection. An adult brain, by contrast, uses the prefrontal cortex for decision-making. The prefrontal cortex is the part of the brain that can reason, analyze, and use good insight,

and, alas, it is not fully endowed with enough myelin until individuals reach their early twenties. It's only then that your son will be able to react less emotionally and more rationally.

So, Mom and Dad, be patient. Your teen is well within his rights to use the ultimate excuse to get away with annoying adolescent behavior: "My brain—or lack of it—made me do that!"

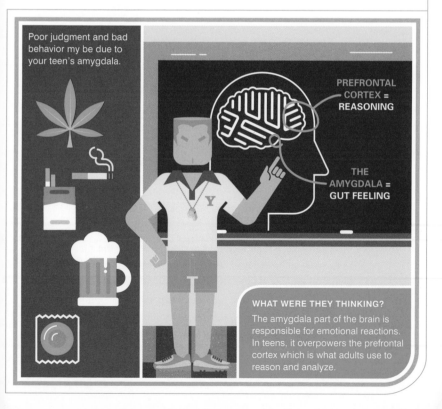

Poor judgment and bad behavior my be due to your teen's amygdala.

PREFRONTAL CORTEX = **REASONING**

THE AMYGDALA = **GUT FEELING**

WHAT WERE THEY THINKING?
The amygdala part of the brain is responsible for emotional reactions. In teens, it overpowers the prefrontal cortex which is what adults use to reason and analyze.

I Was a Teenage Video Addict

Remember Breakout? Or Pong? Those old-school computer games were just the beginning of the electronic game revolution. Games have become far more sophisticated and far more alluring to young teens. These games can also be beguiling to overwhelmed parents because they pacify a child with astonishing ease. Turn on the computer and presto! Instant babysitter.

Three categories of games can suck up large blocks of your child's time, including computer, console, and hand-held types.

■ MMOs ("massively multiplayer online" games) are never-ending, role-playing online computer games that continue whether your teen is logged on or not. Thousands of people can be playing within the universe of an MMO game at one time, and they are highly addictive.

■ Console games, connected to the television, are less interactive but also encourage your child to play for huge blocks of time.

■ Handheld games can be taken anywhere and used anywhere, such as on your family vacation to the Grand Canyon. While you are all slack-jawed over nature's majesty, your teen will be plugging away at her portable video screen.

Video games are seductive: They can be exciting and challenging. They give immediate feedback and are designed for the player to get hooked to advance to the next level or beat a previous score. Kids who are socially phobic or simply socially ill at ease can interact with none of the risks involved in actual face time. But these are hours that ultimately distract your teen from building real-time social skills and emotional connections, playing active sports, enjoying arts, or bonding with family members.

If your child is becoming addicted to video games, he might show signs of isolating himself from old friends in favor of new buddies in the gaming community, giving up favorite hobbies, becoming sneaky about the time he spends playing, jeopardizing relationships with other family members, changing his sleeping and eating habits, skipping school to spend more time on the game, and simply not being able to stop playing or obsessing about the game even though he wants to stop.

Whether your teen is experiencing a full-blown addiction or is wasting more time than he should, you may need to step in.

■ Put firm time limits on gaming, and spell out the consequences when the limit is breached.

■ Install an administrative password so you can monitor and control use of the computer.

■ Install parental-control software that enables you to limit online time and block access to certain sites and games.

■ Make a deal that console cables are handed over only after homework—or whatever else you want done—has been completed.

■ When all else fails, throw the console or cables into the back of the garbage truck on trash day.

Be sure, too, that you model restraint in your own use of electronics. Tear yourself away from that online auction; stop talking on that cell phone, and don't check your e-mail. Your kids are watching!

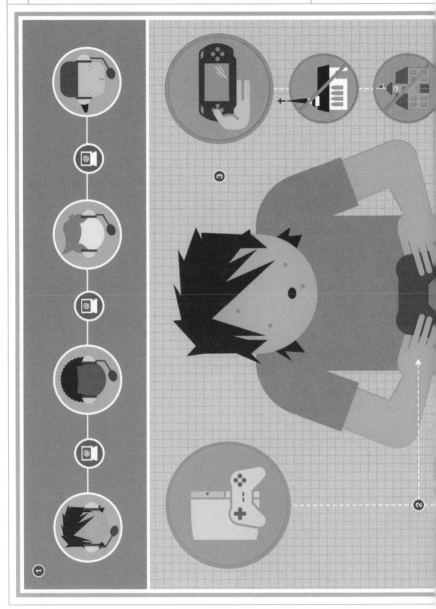

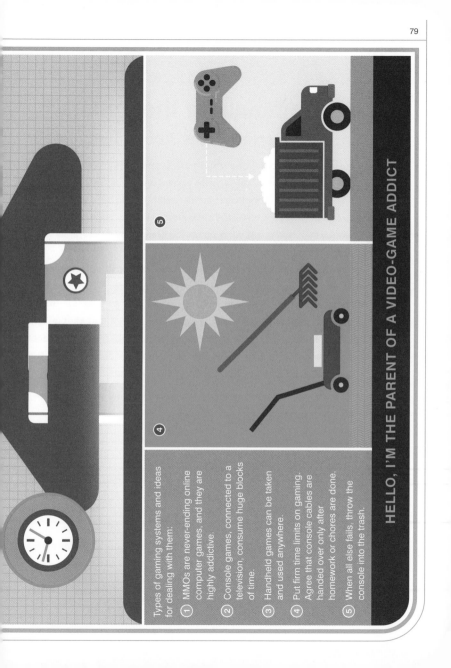

Types of gaming systems and ideas for dealing with them:

1. MMOs are never-ending online computer games, and they are highly addictive.

2. Console games, connected to a television, consume huge blocks of time.

3. Handheld games can be taken and used anywhere.

4. Put firm time limits on gaming. Agree that console cables are handed over only after homework or chores are done.

5. When all else fails, throw the console into the trash.

HELLO, I'M THE PARENT OF A VIDEO-GAME ADDICT

Teen Zombies on the Loose:
What You Need to Know About Teen Sleep

Any parent who's had the opportunity to observe a first period class at their son or daughter's high school knows it isn't an inspiring sight. Classrooms are full of listless, vacant-looking—maybe even sleeping and drooling—zombie children. These kids wish they were back in bed, cozy under the covers, catching up on the sleep they desperately need (between 8½ and 9¼ hours a night, to be precise).

Many parents feel riled up, drained, and resentful after having to endure the strenuous daily morning wake-up routine. "Why can't Sam just go to bed early so he can wake up early? It's so simple!" But as with many of your teenager's annoying habits, it's not that simple, and it's partly a function of his changing body. Sleep debt has a significant impact on a teen's quality of life and therefore the parents', too. But first, let's understand what's going on in the teen body.

Teenage Standard Time

The teen's circadian clock (the body's internal 24-hour clock), which controls periods of sleepiness and alertness throughout its one-day cycle, has begun to shift so that his dip in energy doesn't show up till after you've gone to sleep. It may feel like your teen is living in the next time zone right under your roof. When you are ready to go to bed at the end of the day, he is just revving up, eager for social interactions, music, and computer time. Then in the morning, you wake refreshed and ready to start the day while he is utterly zonked out. Those memories of your kindergartner shouting in the predawn hours from his bedroom, "Mom, is it morning yet?" will seem distant, indeed.

There are a number of factors that can exacerbate this naturally occurring shift in your teen's body clock:

[1] Caffeine intake during the day to counteract the effects of sleep deprivation makes it difficult to settle into a regular sleep cycle.

[2] Stimulating activities that require physical exertion, such as late-in-the-day sports practice or exercise, make it more difficult to wind down.

[3] Watching television, listening to music, and spending time on the computer also make teens more likely to lose track of time and the other visual cues that are associated with bedtime.

[4] The light from all this nocturnal activity in front of the TV or computer is thought to hinder the release of melatonin, a hormone that makes us sleepy.

The changes in a teen's rhythms would be fine if she could sleep until 8 or 9 A.M. the next day. But there's that school thing. So most teens simply begin to accumulate a huge sleep debt that pervades every aspect of their lives as they stay up late and then are forced out of bed in the morning before their bodies have refueled. With many kids getting only six or seven hours of sleep a night, by the end of the week, they might have accumulated ten or more hours of sleep debt.

Sleep deprivation will make a teen:

- moody
- more irritable and aggressive
- less able to concentrate on school and sports performance
- at great risk for driving accidents

⚠️ **EXPERT TIP:** *A drowsy teen who has impaired reaction time and is prone to risk-taking is not the person parents want behind the wheel of a car. You might consider withholding the car keys until your teen builds back sleep reserves.*

Take Back the Night!

It's not easy to convince your son or daughter that he or she will be a better student, athlete, friend, and family member by hitting the pillow by 10 P.M. If sleep habits have gone off the rails for awhile, your child genuinely may not feel drowsy, especially if bolstered by a post-school nap or espresso shot.

Still, you may want to set some ground rules to give your teen a better shot at quality sleep.

[1] Remove the television from the bedroom.

[2] Set an earlier time in the afternoon or early evening to begin homework.

[3] Have a lights-out deadline when computers, cell phones, or anything with a screen must be turned off.

[4] Have your child open the curtains before going to bed so the bedroom is flooded with light in the morning.

[5] Discourage long after-school naps and binge sleeping on weekends, as these further derail normal sleep patterns.

Challenge your teen to try out a healthier sleep schedule for a week or two to see if he or she notices a difference. Feeling recharged,

alert, and emotionally balanced is a pretty persuasive argument, even for a teen.

How to Get Your Teen out of Bed in the Morning

■ Call him on his cell phone. (Funny how his ring tone is always able to penetrate his corpselike sleep.)

■ Arrange to carpool with her crush so she'll be motivated to wake up early to groom and dress with great attention.

■ Give him the Wake-Up Challenge: If he can wake up on time for a week, he gets something he's been lobbying for (pizza dinner on Fridays, more minutes on a cell phone plan, use of the car Saturday night, and so forth).

■ Rustle up something that smells good for breakfast. She won't be able to resist the savory aromas permeating the house.

The Skin Game:
Whiteheads, Blackheads, Acne, and Misery

It does seem unfair. The very morning of your teen's big date, or class photo, or class presentation, she wakes up with a giant pimple on her nose. Oh, the teen years. This most visible consequence of becoming a teen is truly one of the least fun to deal with. Unfortunately, genetics plays a large part in who gets stuck suffering from acne. If you or your spouse had acne, it is likely your kid will, too. Why the skin? Why now? The answers lie in another quick biology lesson about your growing teen:

■ Testosterone levels are high enough now (in boys and girls) that their effects are being visited upon your teen's once-poreless, creamy-perfect skin of childhood.

■ Your child's sebaceous gland will now sporadically go into overdrive, producing too much sebum, a lubricant for the pores. (Stress can also play a role in driving your teen's newly awakened oil-production factory.)

■ Sebum mixes with dead skin cells, which can clog and block the pores.

■ Add in a dash of bacteria to this recipe, and you get those angry red blemishes.

■ Pus results as the body fights the ensuing infection.

It ain't pretty, and it will take some days to resolve.

⚠ *EXPERT TIP: Blackheads are clogged pores that have access to the surface of the skin. Sebum darkens when exposed to oxygen. Whiteheads are clogged pores that are trapped under the surface of the skin. Blackheads and whiteheads go from minor skin irritations to full-blown raging pimples when additional sebum and bacteria build up and inflame the clogged pore. This turn to the dark side is what's known as acne.*

Some Dos and Don'ts

There are some measures your child can take to reduce or at least minimize the effects of acne.

■ Have her wash her face twice a day with a mild cleanser—but beware: Washing too frequently will trigger her skin to produce more lubricating sebum. She should wash and pat skin dry with a washcloth.

■ If your teen needs it, get a little extra firepower with over-the-counter benzoyl peroxide or salicylic anti-acne products. Salicylic acid helps to unclog pores. Benzoyl peroxide removes dead cells from the surface layer of skin, which inhibits blocked sebum. It also kills off bacteria. (BP comes in different strengths, so ask her doctor which strength she should use. Note too that BP makes the skin more vulnerable to sun damage, so your teen will need to take extra care to avoid too much sun exposure.)

■ Direct her to use a moisturizing lotion with the appropriate level of hydration (select a dry, combination, or oily skin formula). She should not let the skin dry out—if it does, it will crank up production of sebum.

■ Make sure she buys makeup labeled "noncomedogenic," which indicates it won't clog pores.

■ Be sure your teen keeps her hands off her face. Although it might seem reasonable to presume that unblocking a blocked pore will help matters, in fact it will only irritate the skin further. No playing with pimples!

DOC TALK: *Remember, it takes time to have a blemish-free face. In today's hurried world, I get calls after only two weeks from teenagers upset that their skin is still pimply. Keep in mind: Acne can get worse before it gets better.*

If your teen doesn't have success with over-the-counter medicines, he'll need to see a dermatologist who can prescribe topical antibiotics or oral medications. These medications are usually taken daily over the course of six months or longer. Other treatments include microdermabrasion and steroidal shots that are administered directly into acne cysts.

Depending on how your teen is faring with acne, he may benefit from talking to a therapist. Many teens can become quite downhearted with recurrent and severe acne, which can affect the child's self-image. Talking with a therapist might give him the additional support he needs during this time.

⚠ DOC TALK: *You should not assume that your teenager is bothered by his or her acne, even if you think it looks bad. Gently probe about his feelings and offer to help him find the medications that can help. However, if he says "leave me alone," then leave him alone. Unless his acne is deeply scarring his face, his pimples are harmless, and it's fine for him to simply learn to live with them.*

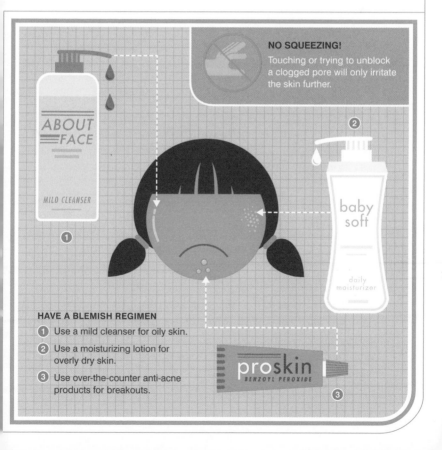

NO SQUEEZING!
Touching or trying to unblock a clogged pore will only irritate the skin further.

ABOUT FACE
MILD CLEANSER

baby soft
daily moisturizer

proskin
BENZOYL PEROXIDE

HAVE A BLEMISH REGIMEN
1. Use a mild cleanser for oily skin.
2. Use a moisturizing lotion for overly dry skin.
3. Use over-the-counter anti-acne products for breakouts.

Feeding Frenzy and the Growing Teen

The teen growth spurt means changing food habits. Simply put, your child will need to increase his caloric intake for his body to grow. Boys tend to require more calories than girls when they are in the prime growing years (between the ages of 14 and 18). Growing boys can take in as many as 4,000 calories a day during big growth spurts and not gain weight, but that's at the far extreme. Teen girls generally should consume around 2,200 calories daily, and teen boys should eat 2,800 calories daily.

How many more calories your teen needs will depend on how active he or she is, but even couch potatoes require more food during the teen years. Now, if you have an Olympian like Michael Phelps (who was eating around 12,000 calories daily while in training) in your house, you will find yourself making many trips to the grocery store to keep up with his demands.

If your son or daughter is concerned about gaining excess weight:

■ Advise steering clear of fast food in favor of eating healthy, home-prepared foods—the less processed, the better.

■ Make eating right easier by stocking up on healthful foods. Make eating a salad with dinner a rule. They're great tummy fillers.

■ Establish the rule that food stays at the kitchen or dining-room table. No little bowls of ice cream or chips sneaking up to the bedroom.

■ Use portion control. Dish out small amounts on small plates.

■ Make sure your teen eats slowly. It takes twenty minutes for the brain to realize the stomach is full.

■ Take care that your child does not skip breakfast.

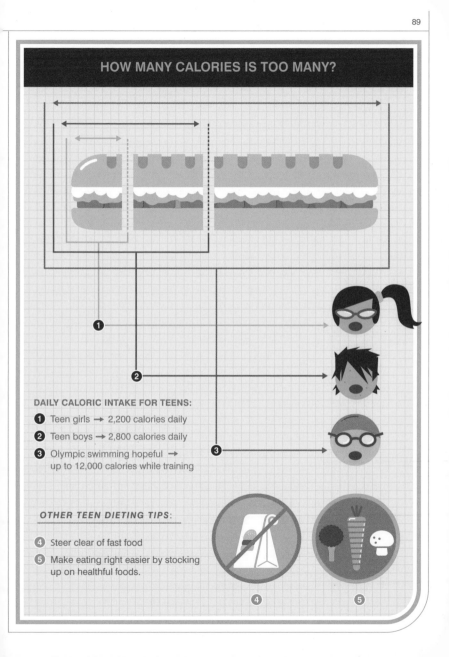

HOW MANY CALORIES IS TOO MANY?

DAILY CALORIC INTAKE FOR TEENS:

1. Teen girls → 2,200 calories daily
2. Teen boys → 2,800 calories daily
3. Olympic swimming hopeful → up to 12,000 calories while training

OTHER TEEN DIETING TIPS:

4. Steer clear of fast food
5. Make eating right easier by stocking up on healthful foods.

⊕ *DOC TALK: In my practice, which specializes in eating disorders, there are three clinical pearls of wisdom I try to pass on to my patients: (1) Fat is not a feeling. When you say, "I feel fat," the hidden message is usually, "I feel lonely," "I feel angry," or "I feel depressed." Focus on the feelings behind the statement. (2) Avoid comments like "That food is bad for me." No food is bad—just less healthy or more healthy. (3) Don't rely on the numbers on a bathroom scale to tell you you're doing the best you can to eat healthy, exercise, and have a strong body image.*

Learning to Love That Bod

It's remarkable to witness the utter self-consciousness of a 12-year-old girl transform into the casual savoir-faire of an 18-year-old strolling around in a bikini. For some kids, it is no big deal growing into their budding adult body. But for others, it can be an awkward, frustrating, and self-critical period of adjustment. Most of us can't claim we're totally at peace with every aspect of our looks as adults, and we've had years to get accustomed to ourselves.

Many girls, in particular, set themselves up for failure by comparing themselves to the models they see in fashion magazines, while many boys obsess over whether they resemble their favorite muscle-bound sports stars. With unrealistic comparisons like these, it's not surprising that only the smallest fraction of teens feel confident about how they stack up. Give your teen a reality check about the process of growing into his or her new body:

■ Many boys who want a ripped bod will have to wait until their bodies start producing high enough levels of testosterone, at around age 16, before they will show any significant muscle growth.

■ Girls will gain weight around the hips and thighs and get curvier as puberty progresses. So many teen girls' ideas about looking like a matchstick waif are unrealistic.

It's All in the Genes—and Then Some

Most teens square out before they stretch out. Just as when they were babies, your kids will seem pudgier before they sprout upward. Genetics play a large part in what your teens look like. It may be tough for a short kid to see his short parents and realize he'll never fulfill his hoop dream of doing a tomahawk jam, or for a girl with tight, curly hair just like her parents' to realize her locks will never blow like silk in the wind. But here's where you get to step in and relay the message that whatever their appearance, your kids should be kind, loving, and accepting of themselves.

It isn't all determined by the genetic roll of the dice, of course. Your children are also picking up on all the messages that you're transmitting—consciously and unconsciously—when it comes to appearance. As a parent, you get to be a powerful role model for self-acceptance. That means you need to resolve your own body image issues before you can expect your child to do so.

■ Be careful about the words you use to describe your personal appearance, as well as your attitude toward what "perfection" looks like.
■ Take special care that your own anxiety over weight and dieting is not conveyed to your teen.

⊕ *DOC TALK: "Honey, we got the letter." Schools are now requiring body mass index (BMI) on school physical forms. Schools then send out letters to families that their child is at risk for being overweight. I strongly believe that these letters are a misguided attempt to help and will serve to label our children. If you get this letter, explain to your child that the number is just a number and that you will talk to your healthcare provider about healthy exercise, healthy eating, and healthy body image.*

Your Body, Your Self

Teens have the uncanny ability to internalize messages even when they're not directed at them. Thus a mom who feels anxious about her own weight or is forever "going on a diet tomorrow" may be telling her daughter that it's okay to obsess over weight gain and physical perfection or that "fat" equals failure or worthlessness. A dad who's constantly ribbing his son over when he's going to develop some "real" muscles might be thinking he's just having some good-natured fun, but there's a good chance he's conveying feelings of negative body image to his child.

EXPERT TIP: *Be aware that the more energy you put into your child's weight loss, the more likely your efforts will backfire and compound the problem. Eating disorder researchers find that this sort of behavior simply puts more negative attention on the issues, to the extent that the teen will struggle with body image and be less likely to have a balanced way of eating and exercising. Some signs your teen may be at risk for an eating disorder include weight loss, regimented dieting, an increase in concern about appearance and whether she looks fat, becoming a vegetarian (which gives the teen a rationale for being rigid around food), social isolation, and excessive exercising.*

Yet some kids will surprise us. Buff jocks may feel terribly lacking, and a teen who falls somewhat short of Adonis will feel 100 percent fine about himself. A kid whose self-esteem is more fragile will tend to get down on

himself over looks, whereas kids with "thicker skin" won't care if they don't look perfect. So don't assume there's a problem if there isn't one. Just be alert to ways to bolster your teen's self-image, and try to help your entire family adopt healthy habits by modeling more healthful attitudes:

- Throw out your bathroom scale.
- Don't diet, but improve your overall approach to health. Exercise regularly, eat more fruits, vegetables, grains, and unprocessed foods, and spend less time in front of the computer and television.
- Avoid junk food and eating at fast food places.
- Educate the family on portion size and balanced meals. Become a family of intuitive eaters. Eat when hungry, not when bored. Stop eating before your stomach feels full.

Though it sounds corny, you need to emphasize that beauty comes in all shapes, sizes, and colors. There's no one definition, and inner beauty is truly the best and longest-lasting attractive attribute.

A Close Shave:
Hair Removal 101

With puberty comes many new adventures, including those of a hirsute nature. Here are some tips for tackling these hairy problems with your teen.

Boy's Edition

Many guys "bug out" with excitement when their peach fuzz finally changes into legitimate shave-worthy growth. Make sure to give your son a lesson on the proper technique for shaving his beard. He'll no

doubt have already spent time in the bathroom observing his dad shave, so he may be pretty familiar with what he's supposed to do. Here are some pointers to review, just in case:

[1] Run a hot shower and steam up the bathroom. The heat will soften the skin and open up pores, making shaving easier.

[2] Make sure the razor has a fresh, clean blade. Old blades can cause uneven shaving or lead to infected hair follicles. Switch blades once a week.

[3] Lather up the face with shaving cream, rubbing it into the skin in a circular motion over all parts you intend to shave. You will know you have applied it correctly when you look like Santa Claus.

[4] Use short strokes. Pull the skin taut with fingers or by flexing muscles for a close, clean shave. Curl lips over teeth when shaving the trickiest spot under the nose. Other facial contortions will give you a flatter, easier surface for shaving.

[5] Rinse the blade with each stroke under running water. Never rush. There's no prize for speed, and haste can lead to nicks and cuts. If you get a cut, staunch the blood flow with tissue and dab on petroleum jelly to help skin heal.

[6] Never go against the grain of hair growth; this can lead to irritated, rashy skin. Hair grows in different directions, so observe your hairs' habits and shave accordingly.

[7] When finished, close up pores by splashing cold water on face. Aftershave can also tighten pores.

[8] Apply shaving balm, gel, or some moisturizer to lubricate the skin.

EXPERT TIP: Electric razors make the job even easier: Steam up the bathroom to open up the pores and soften skin. Keep the surface area dry. Run the razor over the skin according to the manufacturer's directions (each model has different specifications for the razor's optimal shaving technique). Apply moisturizer afterward.

If your son is prone to ingrown hairs (curly whiskers tend to grow back into the skin), he should use a single-blade razor for a shave that's not quite as close. This helps keep the whisker from curling back into the skin as it grows. The final result won't be as smooth, but it will be less bumpy and more comfortable for him—though maybe not for his date.

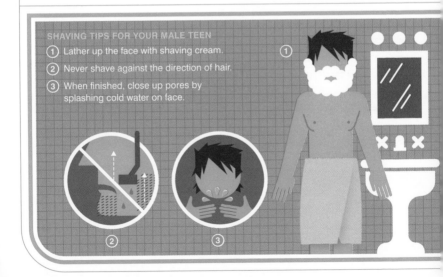

SHAVING TIPS FOR YOUR MALE TEEN
(1) Lather up the face with shaving cream.
(2) Never shave against the direction of hair.
(3) When finished, close up pores by splashing cold water on face.

DOC TALK: *Your teen should never, never share razors. Shared razors mean shared bacteria, and these days some bacteria are getting harder to treat and can spread quickly (for example, MRSA, or methicillin-resistant Staphylococcus aureus). Your teen's skin infections should be examined by his doctor to check for these bacteria.*

Girls' Edition

Girls typically shave armpits and the lower halves of their legs, even though there's no real hygienic reason to do so. Teen girls typically begin to shave when they start to notice their friends doing so, and once their parents give the okay. Just a few general pointers should suffice:

■ For best results, shave in a hot shower.

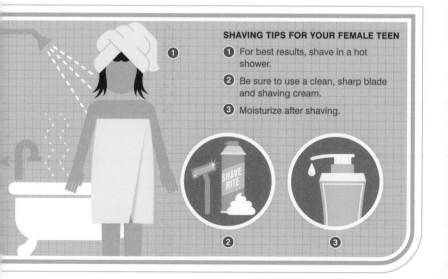

SHAVING TIPS FOR YOUR FEMALE TEEN

1. For best results, shave in a hot shower.
2. Be sure to use a clean, sharp blade and shaving cream.
3. Moisturize after shaving.

- Be sure to use a clean, sharp blade.
- Apply shaving cream to make the process more comfortable.
- Moisturize after shaving.

Teen Obsessives' Edition

Bushy-browed teen girls and boys may ask to borrow your tweezers from time to time to sculpt their eyebrows. Boys in particular may legitimately need some assistance in getting rid of the "unibrow" look. But be aware that modern teens are becoming progressively obsessed with hair removal. Whereas some girls are comfortable with hairy armpits, legs, and pubic areas, others go for the completely denuded look from pit to toe. (Most are somewhere in between.) Boys, too, are feeling the pressure to go hairless. Waxing and shaving backs, stomachs, chests, legs, butts, and even "manscaping" the nether regions are all becoming more common. There is absolutely no medical reason to remove any hair on the body, so this is purely a culturally driven phenomenon.

➕ *DOC TALK: One day I'll write a book titled* Where Has All the Pubic Hair Gone? *I am seeing younger and younger patients who shave or wax their pubic hair. But pubic hair really does serve important functions: It acts like a cushion to protect against injury to the pelvic area and as a barrier against bacteria. Most important, we health-care providers also need to see a teen's pubic hair in order to document the normal development of secondary sexual characteristics.*

FUN WITH FACIAL HAIR

If you want to steer your son away from permanent forays into self-expression like piercings or tattoos, get him interested in having some fun with his facial hair. It doesn't cost a thing, and he can always shave it off when Grandma visits.

MUTTON CHOPS

SPOCK SIDEBURNS

GOATEE

HANDLEBAR MUSTACHE

VAN DYKE

THE AMISH BEARD

THE LUMBERJACK

FU MANCHU

HAZARD

Traditional razors require instruction to prevent shaving mishaps.

[Chapter 3]

School Daze:

Managing Academic Life

Final papers
DUE TODAY!!!

Any family that's experienced bumps in the road over a child's grades, homework struggles, bullies, learning disorders, or stress from college applications knows these woes affect not only the teen but the entire family's happiness quotient. The trick is in how you handle them.

Making the Grade

Realistic expectations will go a long way toward turning down the heat on one of the most common sources of parent-teen conflagrations. Many parents feel powerless and frustrated when their kid comes home with a crummy grade on a paper or a lousy report card. "My kid's smarter than this!" they'll say. You can't go into the classroom and learn for your child, but you also may feel you can't motivate him to stretch for top marks, either.

Another roadblock is your teen's inability to organize himself. It'll be hard for him to do the assignment if he forgot to write it down or bring home the necessary books. Lecturing, shouting, and glaring won't turn that C into an A. So what's a parent to do?

Whose Problem Is This, Anyway?

First you need to make sure you're not trying to fulfill your own failed high-school dreams by living vicariously through your child.

- Becoming a cardiothoracic surgeon may have been your dream, but is it your teenager's?
- Are your expectations appropriate to this particular child?
- Are your expectations high simply because you have another child who is a high achiever?

Each child in a family has her own unique gifts, and they may not necessarily all be the same. But if you've determined that your child's performance is truly not a reflection of your own issues, then by all means, use some careful measures to help your teen close the gap between performance and goal when it comes to making better grades.

Why Are Those Grades Dropping, Really?

Are your child's grades dropping in all subjects or just one particular class? If grades are slipping in all areas, you need to determine whether there are social and emotional issues at work.

■ Is your child beginning to experiment with self-destructive behaviors such as taking drugs, using alcohol, and having risky sex? If so, why?

■ Are your child's sleeping, eating, and social habits changing drastically? She may be depressed and in need of professional help. (If so, you might approach a trusted teacher or school counselor for initial advice.)

■ Is it simply the case that your child is not as motivated to achieve academic success as you want him to be? He might be putting more effort into areas that are more important to him, such as sports, the social scene, or computer games. (Damn you, *World of Warcraft*!)

Another common reason for poor performance is the teen's transition from "lower" to "upper" schools. In the United States, this is the shift from middle school to high school, but in countries throughout the world the timing and nature of the transition may take different forms and, of course, go by different names.

Whatever the case, the shift to upper grades typically brings with it a shift in the model curriculum. In the past, your child may have been taught with a multisensory, hands-on approach that appealed to different learning styles. Upper schools shift the emphasis to a fairly traditional model that features a lecture format, with the teacher as expert. Suddenly, everyone needs to be capable of listening, taking good notes, and absorbing the teacher's lectures. This creates a period of uneasy adjustment for many kids until they master the pertinent skills. Woe to the child with poor listening skills.

Don't Get Angry—Get Help!

Being angry at your child for a poor mark may be a natural response, but it is not a helpful one. Your teen already feels disappointed or negative enough without your throwing emotional kindling into the fire. A more helpful approach might include:

■ Acknowledging that we all make mistakes or get confused.

■ Figuring out specifically why the teen missed certain questions or showed weakness in a graded paper.

■ Using the grade as a "teachable moment." The score highlights what your child didn't master, so now he knows where he needs to improve.

■ Asking your child how he can improve. What methods would work better next time? Does he need to ask for extra help from the teacher or practice certain parts of the lesson more? Would it help if he "played teacher" and retold the lesson to you?

Soon enough, you and your child will begin to see the areas of weakness. Once he knows what he doesn't understand and why, he can begin to fix it. But helping your teen's grades improve is more than simply making sure assignments are completed.

[1] Meet with your child's teacher to discuss the issues. Does he need to improve study skills, get a peer tutor, tape record the lecture for later review, or meet with the teacher during free time?

[2] Review your teen's notebook to see whether he's taking adequate notes. If the notes are okay, he may need better techniques to self-quiz and ensure he understands the material.

[3] If the notes are insufficient, your child may be missing salient lecture points, which will mean he'll score poorly on exams. He can ask to see the teacher's notes, pair up with a partner note-taker to compare notes, or use some computer resources (course companion Web sites or CDs) to better grasp the concepts.

[4] See if a tutor can help your child with organization and reinforce material on a one-on-one basis. (Added bonus: Having a tutor gets you out of unpleasant parent-child power struggles.)

Each of these measures requires commitment and motivation from the student. All the extra support in the world won't help a kid who simply doesn't care!

EXPERT TIP: Is your kid cavalier about bad grades? It might be an indication that he's gone into defensive mode against feeling bad because, in fact, he feels miserable about it. This happens with lots of kids who have undiagnosed learning issues. It's easy to see why they give up: They are disappointed and frustrated and don't have a clue about how to get help. They adopt an attitude of, "Oh, screw it," because it is easier not to care. Not caring protects them from further hurt, embarrassment, and bewilder-

ment. If you suspect this might be the case for your child, be sure to have him screened for learning disabilities. (A more in-depth discussion is on pages 107–109.) Once a kid has customized learning strategies and a curriculum that plays to his strengths and supports his weaknesses, he can experience tremendous progress.

How to Preserve Grades by Conserving Energy

Most teens acquire significant sleep debt each week (see page 80), and many have a hard time ever catching up. A sleepy student is not one who will excel.

Your teen needs around 8½ to 9¼ hours of sleep a night. If she doesn't get that sleep, she may begin to miss school because she's overly tired, and her sleep debt will chronically take away her focus, attention, and good mood. Review the sleep pointers on page 81, but also encourage your teen to reduce her commitments and not fall prey to overscheduling. Many kids have too much homework, and academic stakes are high. Something's gotta give.

Take stock of your teen's schedule and figure out where to decrease the load.

■ Extracurriculars are fun and can enhance a college application, but perhaps this is the year she chooses soccer *or* the debate team, not both.

■ Many kids enjoy part-time jobs, but often the money earned is used for incidentals. What's worth more: A pair of rockin' sneakers or getting top marks? Locking down academic performance is likely to lead to the bigger payoff.

Reality Check:
What If It *Is* a Learning Disorder?

A learning disorder is diagnosed when a child's academic skills are substantially different from what one would expect from the child's aptitude. They often encompass skill areas such as math, writing, or reading (dyslexia), but also include Attention Deficit/Hyperactive Disorder and language disorders.

Many kids with undiagnosed learning disorders put a lot of energy into adaptive strategies, which can carry them through for awhile. But the burden and complexity of academic and social achievement only increases as the years go by, and many such teens will reach a point where they can no longer compensate. You may notice these overt trouble signs:

■ He shows poor academic performance. One of the earliest signals is disorganization, quickly followed by falling grades and anxiety surrounding school.

■ He cultivates a persona. Feeling frustrated and disappointed with his limitations, he may adopt the "class clown" or "rebel with an attitude" persona to save face in front of peers.

■ He's not a full member of the social scene. Kids with Attention Deficit Disorder (ADD), for example, tend to develop emotionally at a slower rate than typical kids. They may avoid social opportunities or be socially inappropriate.

■ He can't keep up with conversational flow. He becomes frustrated and shut-down or physically aggressive.

■ His home life goes haywire. Teens who have worked so hard all day to keep it together at school may come home moody, irritable, or belligerent. Every kid can have a rough day, but consistently negative behavior is not typical.

Teens with learning disorders can also be at higher risk for depression and risky behaviors, as well as for being bullied.

You may have a difficult task teasing out a learning disorder from everyday adolescent angst, lack of academic motivation, or a temporary hiccup.

[1]   Start by calling a trusted teacher to see if anything feels "off."

[2]   Make an appointment with your child's pediatrician or a specialist (often recommended by the pediatrician) who works with clients your child's age.

[3]   If the specialist recommends getting a psychoeducational evaluation, schedule one as soon as possible. This evaluation, performed by an educational or school psychologist, provides a thorough learning and emotional profile of the child through medical and school histories, teacher and parent impressions, and results from a battery of tests.

[4]   If the test results confirm learning issues, your child will typically receive an individualized educational plan that maps out next steps in detail.

[5]   You may choose to place your child in a school that caters to his or her particular learning differences, or to supplement current schooling with occupational or speech and language therapy, social skills groups, or other programs.

Getting the needed services can be life-changing for your child and your family. Properly treated, kids with learning issues often find passions to pursue that offset the negative experiences. They find a community of teens who share their interests. Once they can put their

energy and love into what they are good at, the challenges they face daily will diminish proportionally.

⚠ **EXPERT TIP:** *Be sure to let your teen in on every step of the process so that he doesn't project a far worse situation than truly exists. It's important to keep him informed and positive.*

Home Is Where the Homework Is

Some kids haphazardly attack homework assignments with no real method. They know how to get by until the workload increases to a breaking point, when they just can't "wing it" any longer. This is when you can step in to help your child get some structure.

It's All in the Habits

[1] It may seem pretty obvious, but make sure your teen copies down the correct assignments in one place, whether an assignment book or to-do list, and brings home all necessary books and study materials.

[2] If she has a tendency to have a chaotic locker and disorganized life, get her in the habit of double-checking that her bookbag has all the things she needs before she leaves school.

[3] Set up a regular homework time so she doesn't procrastinate, forget, or promise to get to it later. If she gets home before you do, give her a specific program to follow. Tell her she can fix a snack and relax, and then begin

homework at 4 P.M. Let her know that you'll be calling about that time to remind her to stay on track (in a non-nagging way, of course!).

[4] Set up a regular homework station where she can concentrate. Many kids study while their instant messaging is up, with music or television going full blast—not a great atmosphere for working with quiet, sustained focus. And if your teen insists on "working" while flopped out on her bed, she's likely to fall asleep. She should sit at a table where she can spread out her materials, with her feet touching the floor. Keeping her feet on the floor can be "grounding" and will help her stay organized.

[5] Determine whether your child works better with silence or background music. Without music, some kids get too distracted by other ambient sounds in the house.

[6] Have your teen take a moment before plunging in to map out her plan of attack. Hardest jobs should come first, when she has the most energy, but if she's feeling fidgety, she can start off with an easier assignment to get her momentum going.

[7] Let her take a short break after a long period of work. She may want to stretch her legs, do some stomach crunches, get the blood pumping, and then hunker down again before too much time elapses. Each child is different: Some can work for a two-hour stretch, whereas another may be able to focus for only thirty minutes at a time.

[8] Get your teen in the habit of keeping an assignment calendar at home. This will give her a visual aid and also let you know when to offer a gentle reminder about a long-term assignment.

⚠ **EXPERT TIP:** *Help your child "chunk" the work for a big paper or project so that she can manage a bearable workload until it's done. She can tackle a portion every weekend leading up to the due date. Leaving a major assignment until the night before can be a major stressor, but finishing a big project early is a fantastic feeling. If your teen experiences this one time, she will be motivated to aim for early completion next time.*

[9] Check in with your child each day to monitor her progress. You can offer assistance, answer questions, or determine whether she needs to ask the teacher follow-up questions on the material.

✚ **DOC TALK:** *Remember that organizing and managing short-term and long-term homework projects require some of those "executive function" skills that are among the last to mature in the teenage brain (see page 73). Knowing this may give you just a bit more sympathy for what your teen is going through.*

To Supervise or to Meddle?

Some parents wonder how involved they should be with homework. Should the teen "own" his homework challenge all by himself, or should the parents supervise each session daily? The middle ground between these two extremes seems most practical and realistic. But an entirely hands-off approach would suit only the rare, highly motivated and responsible teen.

[1] If your child is struggling with homework, put him on notice: He can handle his homework solo for two or three days, but if you start to see problems, you are going to step in.

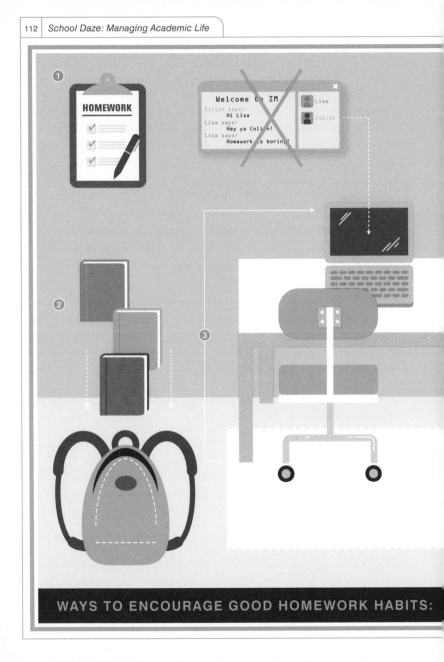

WAYS TO ENCOURAGE GOOD HOMEWORK HABITS:

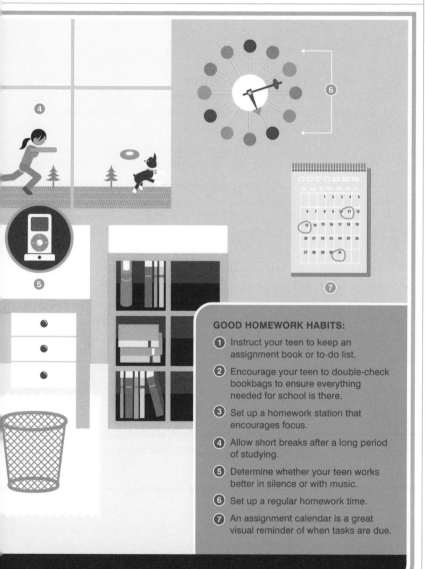

GOOD HOMEWORK HABITS:

1. Instruct your teen to keep an assignment book or to-do list.
2. Encourage your teen to double-check bookbags to ensure everything needed for school is there.
3. Set up a homework station that encourages focus.
4. Allow short breaks after a long period of studying.
5. Determine whether your teen works better in silence or with music.
6. Set up a regular homework time.
7. An assignment calendar is a great visual reminder of when tasks are due.

ing teens a place where they can focus on homework is crucial to academic success.

[2] Specify the period of time—say, two weeks—during which you will be monitoring his every homework move. Then back off and see whether he's learned to organize his work. Most kids will be motivated to escape your oppressive presence.

[3] Do your best to help your child put his good studying habits to work (see page 109).

[4] Help him use some of the newer technology tools to keep on top of assignments. Many schools have homework Web sites where teachers post assignments daily. You can check in, too, to make sure your teen is completing them. Additionally, some schools put the teacher's password-protected grade book online.

It's simply unrealistic to expect a 12-year-old to manage his homework load by himself, but as your teen gets older, you should be able to step back and play a much smaller role in helping him plan, organize, and complete assignments.

Performance Anxiety:
Helping Your Kid Handle Stress

Your daughter walks into the room and is practically hyperventilating as she lists all the tests, papers, parties, study groups, sports practices, and college prep tests she must complete or participate in—not to mention that she must, must, MUST get her hair highlighted this week or she won't be able to show her face at school. The thought crosses your mind that if you don't get her a paper bag to breathe into, she might just

faint. This is likely not a full-blown panic attack, but just the common sight of a teen feeling overwhelmed.

Breathing Is Fundamental

Stress and anxiety are frequent visitors to the teenage psyche. Teens have high expectations for themselves, and they want to impress peers, parents, and teachers. Some students are gripped by the financial realities that they have to do well to get a scholarship if they hope to go to college. Some parents emphasize good grades incessantly. Some kids feel academic pressure more keenly because they have underlying learning issues that haven't been pinpointed.

Here are some of the warning signs that the anxiety is more than the garden-variety stress:

- Excessive irritability
- Isolation, secrecy
- Physical complaints: headache, stomachache, fatigue
- Change in eating or sleeping habits
- School avoidance
- Letting loose on the teen party scene; binge drinking on a regular basis
- Disruption of family life (Your teen's stress is infiltrating all aspects, with turmoil and heightened tension that does not abate.)
- Dramatic changes in behavior (Your formerly introverted child is talking back, lashing out, and having emotional eruptions; or, conversely, your normally outgoing child is shutting down.)

And here's what you can do about it:
- Problem solve: If your child is battling a particularly difficult class, help

him brainstorm solutions. (See "Making the Grade, "page 102, for ideas.) Having a plan will go a long way toward reducing anxiety.

■ Use the power of positive thinking: Help him stamp out black-and-white thinking and drama spirals. Reassure your child that if he gets a bad mark, it's not the end of the world. Even if he gets only a 3.0 average when he desperately worked for a 3.75, tell him he can still get into a college that will make him happy.

■ Change your attitude: Parents can create problems by emphasizing grades rather than the learning process and the skills that go along with acquiring knowledge. Allow your child to try to resolve situations herself. It can take your teen time and practice before these skills are in place. When they are, her grades will reflect that.

■ Give the child "permission" to have a hard time: Screeching "Why is this happening?" doesn't set a tone of acceptance. It will only make your teen feel worse. The more he experiences compassion, the more he'll try to do his best. Criticizing will only make him internalize negativity.

■ Find your child a mentor: Your teen may find some relief by talking with an older cousin or a trusted adult who can listen sympathetically.

■ Get your kid some exercise: Tell her to go for a run or shoot some hoops—any sort of physical exertion intense enough to release those relaxing, happy hormones known as endorphins.

■ Get your teen to vent with some talk therapy: Contact the school counselor or a therapist to help your child understand her emotional landscape.

■ Get some comic relief: Rent some comedies to lighten up the mood. *Simpsons*, anyone? *The Daily Show*? *30 Rock*?

■ Let your child get help by giving help: Volunteering to help someone in need—whether by working in a soup kitchen or cleaning up an abandoned lot—will give your teen a sense of the larger world beyond her immediate problems. She will be appreciated, and that always feels good.

■ Teach stress-management skills: Teach him guided imagery and deep-breathing or deep-muscle relaxation techniques. These work just as well for working up the nerve to ask out a prom date as for dealing with mortgage payments. Once teens learn about the mind-body connection, they can use these skills throughout their lives.

■ Make sure you have a good time together. Remind him that school and grades are a *part* of his life, but not everything.

Bullies, Mean Kids, and Hurt Feelings

Not every kid has an archenemy á la Lex Luthor at school, but for many parents it can sure feel that way. There's always that one obnoxious kid we wish would move to the other side of the country, or whose parents we dream would jump onboard the home-schooling movement, and quick. Alas, dealing with mean kids is part of growing up and learning how to live in an imperfect world.

How to Recognize a Bully

Disrespectful comments, impulsive rudeness, or even a heated argument aren't bullying, even though they can still hurt your child's feelings. Parents can help coach children in these matters. Bullying, though, is more systematic and corrosive than a one-time rude comment. It's when a group of children or one ringleader singles out a weaker, more vulnerable child and harasses him on an ongoing basis either verbally, physically, or emotionally.

A bully is not fighting to hash out differences and move on, but to make the weaker child suffer, and to make himself feel more powerful.

But unlike Superman, the child who is bullied has no superpowers to defend himself and, if the bullying continues, he'll begin to internalize the notion that he deserves to be the target.

Bullying should be taken very seriously. A victimized child can experience poor academic performance, anxiety, depression, self-destructive behaviors, and suicidal thoughts. Not to mention, the perpetrators are often in certain need of therapy themselves.

Shining a Light on the Bully

Many kids who are bullied are ashamed to tell their parents. This is a sizable obstacle if your teen is reluctant to discuss the situation or if he flat-out denies it. You will need to take action if you notice your child

- becoming more irritable.
- isolating her- or himself from friends and family.
- acting depressed.

It may be hard to interpret these behaviors when you have little more than your gut to go on, but try to open lines of communication with your child using "fact-based" conversation starters. "I've noticed you've been spending a lot of time alone in your room. Is there something on your mind?" Use the informal parental phone network and probe what others might know about your child's situation.

When your child does open up, he may say he wants to handle the situation himself. He may be afraid of greater repercussions if adults get involved. He might be hoping it will "all go away," or he may feel so isolated that he can't even conceive that others can help. Give him the chance to fix the situation, with the caveat that you reserve the right to intervene if it appears not to be working. If he is getting physically hurt, however, you need to move in immediately to ensure your child is kept safe. Fighting can easily escalate when adults are not present to intercede. And no, a little bit of trouble from the other boys will not "toughen" him up.

⊕ DOC TALK: *I encourage teens to come up with their own solutions, but when you leave your teen alone with a problem, be sure to identify a specific time frame for checking back in: an hour, a day, or a week. Then don't forget to follow up. This shows your teen that you respect his efforts, but that you are ready to help out at a moment's notice.*

Get the School Involved

Contacting the bully's parents directly is never a good idea. Most parents are very defensive of their children, and being told that your child is a bully does not tend to bring out the best conflict-resolving responses.

[1] Call the school counselor, psychologist, or other support staff, who should be familiar with and trained in these sorts of situations. An engaged teacher may be able to help as well.

[2] Work together with the staff to help your child form an action plan. He can

■ confront the bully by standing tall and calmly telling him to stop. (Many bullies count on the victim's and onlookers' passivity.)
■ use humor or quick wit to defuse confrontations.
■ walk away and simply not engage with or acknowledge the bully.
■ enlist the help of friends to support him and shout down a bully's bad

behavior. (Two kids will have a better chance to shift the balance of power, and a friend can also help build up your child's confidence after an unpleasant confrontation.)

You can role-play the action plan so your teen keeps his wits about him when the bully makes his move.

[3] Let the counselors step in to provide emotional support for your child and help examine the situation more closely. A counselor can point out that even if there's some truth to the bully's words, so what? He can help the child to be comfortable with who he is.

[4] Create a nest of support for your child to let him feel that he is well liked, respected, and loved. A nurturing home life will protect your teen from many of adolescence's bumps and trials.

[5] Help your child establish friendships by getting involved in activities he enjoys. When children feel good about their social skills, they feel good about themselves. That's the best protection from bullying and negative behavior.

DOC TALK: *I tell parents to be on the lookout for bullying behaviors. Male bullying tends to be physical, flagrant, and more likely to escalate. Female bullying is more emotional, more insidious, and more secretive. In the latter case, the "alpha" girl stands at the epicenter of a social web and casts her mighty power over the weaker girls in the group.*

D: AVOIDANCE

What the Experts Say

The following essential tips will help you further understand teen bullying and its mediation:

■ Direct conflict mediation, where both parties sit in the same room and tell their sides of the story, does not work. In fact, it often allows for the child to be victimized by the bully all over again. Parents should never agree to this arrangement.

■ If school personnel are not receptive to or act dismissive of your attempts to counter a bully, you may have to rally other parents to your cause. It's in the best interest of all families to make sure the school does not tolerate bullying, and that a culture of cruelty inside and outside the classroom is not perpetuated.

■ The bystander category is where most kids are likely to find themselves when another child is bullied. Parents need to teach children to squelch mean behavior and not be passive. Both bystanders and victims should know they can ask adults for help.

■ Bullying and ordinary teenage social drama crop up more frequently in early and middle adolescence. By the time teens are in the final stage of adolescence, they've figured out how to shut down bullying or have sorted out the social hierarchies that were so vital earlier. Mean behavior also evolves as the years go by, moving from name calling in the hallways and shunning in the cafeteria to gossip, social exclusion, and malicious online chats, three-way setup phone calls, instant messaging, and texting. Home schooling, here we come!

Handling the Car Pool Brat

Now that you've dealt with the serious issues of schoolyard bullying, it's time to turn to the more mundane and yet perhaps more entertaining irritant of life with teenagers. Inevitably, when it comes to having teens, you will find yourself pulled into a league of carpooling parents. And just as inevitably, you will be forced to contend with someone else's vociferously obnoxious kid. Here's how to deal with the situation:

- Turn up the music on the car radio.
- Buy an engrossing book on CD that you will all enjoy. It will cut down on the chatter, and everyone can learn something along the way.
- Offer to provide breakfast in the car and hand out granola bars, juice boxes, and so forth. Anything that will keep that teen's mouth busy but not talking.
- If the teen is a talker or not shy about offering up opinions, pose a few well-timed questions to get loose lips dishing on all the things your own kid won't share.
- If the child's behavior is simply beyond tolerance, tell her parent that you will have to take a break from carpooling for a month—maybe two.

Of course, if you choose to take the high road, you can always:

- Let your child handle the other teen's obnoxious behavior, but use it as a "teaching moment."
- Later in the day, review and analyze the conversation with your teen.
- Try to understand the other child's point of view and think of the reasons she says the things she does.
- Talk about strategies that can shut down irritating conversations.

Ready or Not:
Time to Think About College

It may seem crazy to start thinking about college when your daughter is still in a training bra or your son is in braces, but the distant drumbeat of higher education—and in the United States, at least, the college application process—can already be heard. Whether taking preliminary college exams, beefing up coursework to look good to a particular school, or simply making visits to local campuses and schools, teens are getting serious about the process earlier and earlier.

■ Aside from signing up for tests and prep courses for them, your teen should be thoughtful about her course load, taking any necessary classes that will set her up to apply for the type of program she is interested in. If she's set her heart on studying economics, she will need to take some advanced mathematics classes. If she's determined to be a graphic designer, she may want to take elective courses in the visual arts to build an impressive portfolio. Having a unique talent or experience is another way to set a student apart from the pack of college applicants. (Glockenspiel, anyone?)

■ Get your child thinking and visualizing herself at college. Help her determine the kind of setting that's the most appealing. Urban, suburban, or rural? Local or across the country? Small or massive? Bohemian, no-nonsense, or trade oriented?

■ Help her find universities or colleges that are known for the specialty she wants to pursue.

■ Sign her up with a counselor who can help her apply to the schools she's most interested in.

■ Be sure to give her some healthy perspective. In particular, never use the term "dream school" within her earshot. There is no one perfect school for any child. Allowing a child to fixate on a "Holy Grail" school can lead to heartbreak.

EXPERT TIP: *You may be tempted to commandeer the school application process, since you know it's riddled with deadlines, fees, and preparation. But your child should be steering the ship. Buy her a calendar and help her fill in the deadlines for tests; requests for teacher recommendations, transcripts, and applications; and interviews. Once she's been accepted to a number of schools, you can set the financial parameters, but the selection of the college should ultimately come from your teen.*

Road Tripping and Campus Visits

The campus visit is very influential in your teen's decision-making process. Yet the reasons a school is suddenly "off the table" or shoots to number-one status often have very little reason behind them.

It may be exasperating to parents when teens start acting like feng-shui experts, basing a thumbs-up or thumbs-down on such ephemera as campus layout, a dorky tour guide, the campus's lack of trees, the campus's overabundance of trees, or an overnight host who was too emo, too gangsta, too hipster, or too nerdy. Bad weather or too-many-tours-in-a-row exhaustion can all affect the teen's impression.

■ Keep tours to one school a day, ideally. Two are manageable, but any more than that can become unproductive.

■ You might be tempted to bring younger siblings, but they often become bored and can detract from your special time with the older child.

■ If you feel your kid's impression of a school is unjustified, remind him that a dreary day or a pompous tour guide should not be the sole reason to condemn an entire institution. Take another look at the curriculum together, and remind him that he shouldn't choose a school based on the landscaping.

■ If your teen previously thought the school would be the best match, consider a return visit another time. Or set up a meeting with a professor in the field your child wants to pursue.

■ To stave off a homogenous glazing-over, have your teen write down impressions in a journal immediately after each visit. This will help when he's back home and has to decide which ones he will continue to pursue.

In the end, however, you must respect your child's instincts. Some of your own major decisions—whom you sought out for dates, what college you picked, which home you bought—were no doubt also rooted in some gut-level intuition. Be aware that you still exert a lot of influence over your child, so try not to sway him with your own impressions of a school.

■ Bite that lip on the drive home, and let your child do the talking. This is particularly important if the child is visiting your or your spouse's alma mater.

■ Refrain from trips down memory lane, singing the school "fight" song, or any other types of nostalgia. If the kid hates the school, he's put in an awful spot. He'll feel he is rejecting you if he rejects the school.

■ Make schools with family connections last on the tour list so that your child can be open to new schools.

Some things to keep in mind when visiting colleges with your teen:

1. Remind your teen that bad weather shouldn't cause him or her to write off a college.

2. Have your teen keep a journal to record each college visit.

3. Don't take a trip down memory lane if you are visiting your alma mater.

4. Younger siblings can ruin a trip if they become bored.

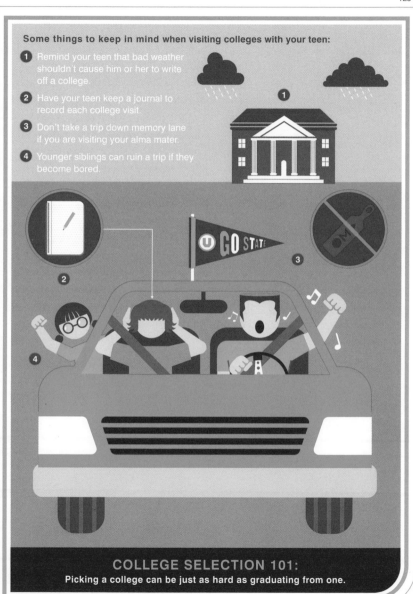

COLLEGE SELECTION 101:
Picking a college can be just as hard as graduating from one.

Chapter 4

Social Studies:

Your Teen's Scene

Fitting in, being well liked and accepted, and finding a "tribe" to belong to are of paramount importance to your teen. She is now acutely aware of the social implications of what she does in front of her peers, whether it's raising a hand in class or sitting next to the school's alpha girl in the lunchroom. By the time the teenage years hit, friendship translates into membership, self-esteem, and self-definition.

Consciously or not, your teen is working to establish and hold on to her rank in the school's unofficial social registry. You might be puzzled by how much energy she puts into making and maintaining friendships, but the easiest way to create her own identity and separate from her parents is by bonding with her chosen herd.

You Are No Longer the Center of Your Child's Universe

From ages 11 to 13, "tweens" still rely on their parents for comfort even as they get increasingly involved in the complex social world. Full-fledged teenagers, though, begin to invest their emotional lives in their friends, replacing the role their parents used to fill. His friends are now the ones who provide security. Yes, you may feel uncomfortable being downgraded to the B team, but your teen is actually showing a healthy and natural progression in his social relationships. (And the upside to feeling increasingly nonessential to your teen is that you may experience a rekindling of intimacy with your partner as you both become less kid-centered.)

■ As your teen moves to late adolescence, he'll disengage from the big groups and segue into closer individual relationships, sometimes through dating or culling his herd of friends down to a few good ones.

■ As he progresses through the teen years, he'll develop enough ego strength to thrive as an individual, without relying solely on parents or friends to define who he is.

All of the energy invested into friend management and relationship grooming actually helps the process of self-discovery and maturation, even though it seems like one big headache from the parental perspective.

Child Abandonment Syndrome:
Parents' Edition

As he expresses his autonomy from family during midadolescence, you will know your child less than you ever have. His emotional distance will be matched by physical distance, too. He won't want to be seen with you if he can avoid it, especially when friends might be nearby. It's hard to project coolness in front of your friends when your mom is asking for a kiss goodbye at the bus stop. Parents are advised to respect this increasing desire for space whenever possible. Be prepared:

■ The intensity of your involvement in his life will naturally diminish.
■ He will keep secrets and feel more comfortable expressing emotions and opinions with his buddies rather than with his dear old mom and pop.
■ His natural inclination will be to keep his private thoughts on the down-low, since he believes parents just don't understand.

Quite often, kids are correct about their assessment of their social scene. You have not observed the million and one interpersonal school moments enough to appreciate what your child's social scene is like.

Yet despite being clueless, you can still remind your kid about your willingness and availability to listen and connect. A parent who can be a good sounding board is particularly important as friends quickly come in and out of your child's life.

[1] As he tries to figure out where he belongs, he may hang on tenuously to one group, switch to another group voluntarily, or get unceremoniously dropped from the group he wants to be with. All of this turmoil can unleash some intense emotions that need to be vented to a safe and understanding parent.

[2] To stay connected, make your house the central hub for your teen's friends. If your house is the hangout joint, you'll be better able to get a sense of the teenager's life. A well-stocked refrigerator and snack cabinet can help keep those hungry teens coming back. (Most teens have a hard time resisting an unlimited supply of chips.)

[3] Offer to be the driver to social destinations—school functions, sports practice, and the like. Listening quietly from the front seat is a fruitful method for gathering all the latest teen gossip and hearing what's on their minds.

⊕ *DOC TALK: If you are "overhearing" conversations, kindly refrain from comments, suggestions, or criticisms. If you continue to listen, you will acquire much more insight into your teen's life and you will be better prepared to help when help is asked for.*

The Truth About Cliques

Your child's cliques began back in the days of all those mommy groups and neighborhood potlucks you used to attend together during his infanthood and toddlerdom. The difference during the preteen and teen years is that moms and dads are no longer calling the play-date shots. Your teen isn't hanging out with a group of kids just because the moms are all friends. Now she's making the selections and changing the groupings as she sees fit. Certainly factors like familiarity, geographical proximity, and similar interests play a part in her choices. But just because two girls are on the lacrosse team and live on the same street does not guarantee that they will be hanging out together.

Charisma, social skills and maturity, self-confidence, humor, smarts, wealth, looks, family status, and athletic ability can all factor into social pecking orders. The best you can hope for is that you've instilled enough values in your child that she'll pick good friends for the right reasons.

Running with the In Crowd

Cliques are not all bad. A band of friends can provide support, fun, intellectual and social stimulation, and a place to assert a blossoming self-identity without fear of rejection or humiliation.

But some kids are more susceptible to the creepier social machinations that can run amok during the early teen years. Gossiping, name-calling, rumor-mongering, and exclusionary practices are just some of the unpleasant aspects of life inside a clique. In this environment, lonely or shy kids run the risk of being coerced to drink or try drugs or cigarettes just to be included and not shunned.

SITTING WITH THE "IN" CROWD: Fitting in with the right crowd is important

teens. Instilling values in your children will help them pick good friends for the right reasons.

■ If your teen chooses to confide in you when she's distressed over a social blowup with friends, your first reaction should simply be to listen and acknowledge what she's feeling.

■ Teens complain most about meddling moms and dads. Don't fall into that trap. Your kid just wants to vent. Instant problem-solving for her is not the remedy for her hurt feelings.

■ Let her tell her story, again and again. The hurt will likely linger, but now she knows she has a parent who will support her and respect her feelings.

■ Learning to cope with the hurt will build resilience. It's hard to stand by passively, but in the long run she needs to go through the process in order to grow.

■ After some time has passed and your teen has gone beyond the initial flurry of emotions, you can help her problem-solve a way to handle the situation.

⊕ *DOC TALK: Before you give advice or make comments, simply ask your teen, "Would you like my suggestions or my advice?" This approach reinforces your respect and trust in allowing her to problem-solve. If she says no, respond with a simple, "I am always here if you want some help."*

Mean Girls, Inscrutable Boys:
Meet the Stereotypes

Girls have the reputation of generally being more "clique-y." They're the friend collectors who strive to be where the social buzz is, and they tend to be more exclusionary when it comes to maintaining their posse.

Boys have the reputation of generally being more content with having a few good friends and not over-thinking their social status. When boys have a conflict, they tend to deal with it and move on—or not deal with it and move on. The difference between the sexes may be that boys simply have weaker verbal communication skills or that society expects them to be less emotional about their feelings.

In the early teen years, boys tend to spend a lot of energy posturing competitively with each other. Teasing, blunt name-calling, and physical aggression are common. Older boys typically outgrow fighting.

Whether your teen is a boy or a girl, encourage the cultivation of friends from different social groups and activities. If your teen has friends in different circles, she can always hop to another bunch of friends when trouble arises without having to worry about being ostracized or isolated.

Bad to the Bone?

The teenage years are a time for experimentation. So if your teen is hanging out with an undesirable crowd, don't panic. It may be just a passing thing. Teens try out different allegiances as they try out different personas. And even when a child spends time with a rougher lot, that doesn't mean she'll take on their behaviors (at least not permanently).

[1] Think carefully before drawing conclusions about your child's "wrong" friends. The kid with the tattoos and piercings could be quite supportive of your child, whereas the straight-laced, clean-cut kid may be introducing your kid to dangerous situations. The best rule of thumb: Look at actions and behaviors, not outward appearances.

[2] Always tread softly when questioning your child's choice of friends. Overt lobbying from you will almost surely backfire and drive your teen even more firmly into the group of kids you dislike.

[3] Accept the fact that you are no longer the primary organizer of your child's social life. All you can do is raise the issue as a way for her to think over the pros and cons of spending time with a certain crew.

[4] Ask your teen to explain what she likes about these friends. You'll both get a better understanding of the thought process behind her choices.

[5] Reinforce for your child that she does have choices. You can try to set basic limits, give recommendations, and suggest activities that would naturally steer her away from the "bad crowd," but in the end your teen is likely to find a way to do what she wants. The most you can do—and you should start to do so well before she reaches her teens—is to foster an environment of open and frank communication.

[6] Acknowledge that you're on the same page: You all want her to be independent. But what will help you be more comfortable with her independence is seeing her make good choices, showing good judgments, and coming to you to discuss things when she needs to.

⊕ *DOC TALK: What to say when your teen wants a tattoo or body piercing? (1) Wait a day to collect your thoughts. (2) Figure out what's motivating him, how serious he is, what his plan for getting one is, and whether he knows the risks. (3) Wait a day to decide what to say, talking it over with your partner, pediatrician, and other parents. (4) If you decide to let him go ahead, do some research to find the safest place for getting a tattoo or piercing. (5) Finally, resist the urge to say "I told you so" when the piercing gets infected or he wishes he never got the tattoo. From the medical perspective, I discourage tattoos because of their permanence, the risk of infection, the not-infrequent regret later in life, and the costly price of removal. I try to identify alternatives that will help teens achieve their goal (i.e., hair coloring, henna tattoos, etc.). Piercings tend to be slightly less risky but still carry the risk of infection and scarring.*

Tech Talk:

How to Keep Your Teen Safe in Cyberspace

As a parent of a teen, you have a distinct disadvantage in this age of ever-evolving technology. You haven't lived through the temptations and dangers of cyberspace, so you can only guess at what might be dangerous for your children. Back in your day, crank-calling the cutest girl or guy in class and hanging up might have been the extent of your technological indiscretions. Nowadays pornography, child predators, cyber-bullying, and rumor-mongering are all only a click away.

Resolving not to have a computer in the house won't solve the problem. Teens can access computers at school, at friends' homes, and at cafés, and they can also get Internet access on cell phones.

There are a lot of factors that conspire to make teens particularly vulnerable to misusing or overusing these shiny techno-toys:

- Impulsiveness
- Lack of maturity
- Minimal sense of consequences
- Sexual curiosity coupled with insecurity

Remember, your teen's prefrontal cortex, the seat of higher reasoning and judgment, doesn't mature until the final stage of adolescence, making her particularly vulnerable to the many engaging images and other lures online. It's time to have some forthright conversations together.

Prevention Is the Best Medicine

More likely than not you've already had to set limits on media throughout your child's life. What movies can she see? What television shows is he mature enough to watch? But the stakes change with the Internet since the risks of harm are higher.

[1] Talking candidly to your child about the time she spends online.

[2] Set some thoughtful limits on computer and phone use. Make sure she never drives and texts at the same time, for example, and doesn't spend all of her free time in front of the computer.

[3] Make sure she understands that no communication (texting, e-mailing, conversations in chat rooms or social networking sites, posts to online journals or blogs) is private, and that everything can easily be made public.

■ That e-mail to her best friend about why she hates the math teacher can be forwarded directly to the math teacher.
■ Naughty photos sent by e-mail to her boyfriend (called "sexting") might end up being sent to the entire school. This "sexting" is of great concern; disciplining the offenders may involve criminal pornography charges.
■ Blog posts about all the beer and pot she consumed at the Valentine's Day dance can be read by admissions officers at the college she's applying to.

[4] The best rule your teen should learn is to ask herself, before she hits "send": Would I feel comfortable if my [grandmother, favorite teacher, rabbi, parent, headmaster, etc.] read this e-mail, blog entry, or text? Tell her to imagine that posting to a social networking site or blog is like having her message appear on a billboard at the side of the highway. It can be read by anyone.

EXPERT TIP: *It might boggle your mind to learn that your kid feels no shame about broadcasting questionable behavior far and wide over the Internet. He may even, after some open conversation, confess that these posts make him feel cool. Try to give him some guidance so he can better understand the consequences. You don't have to act like a prosecuting attorney; just show that you are genuinely curious about his point of view and confident that he'll figure out the best course of action.*

Trust, but Verify

Adults know that much information available on the Internet is unreliable. It's important that you teach your teen to be skeptical about what he reads and with whom he comes in contact online.

- Be sure he checks and double-checks any information found online.
- Encourage him to speak to you about things he reads and sees while surfing the Net.
- Make sure he's aware that people online can pose as somebody they're not. Adults can create teen identities, and kids can create false identities to pose as other classmates—or even teachers.

Sexual Predators on the Prowl

Anonymity on the Net means duplicity runs rampant, and it's a grim fact: Sexual predators lurk on chat rooms frequented by teens. To make sure your teen is not victimized:

[1] Set clear rules for time spent in chat rooms.

[2] Make sure your child knows not to divulge any personal information to anyone online (including passwords, names, address, school, age, or ways to be contacted).

[3] Be sure she knows to report anyone attempting to arrange a face-to-face meeting.

[4] Be sure to save all suspicious communications in the event you need to prove wrongdoing in court.

[5] If your child gets into trouble after visiting a forbidden site, be sure to be supportive. Instead of blaming her, applaud her for confessing and asking you for help. The same way you lavish praise on a dog that returns home after escaping out the front door, reinforce what she's done right.

⚠ *EXPERT TIP: Be aware! A cyber bully can use personal information to pose as your teen and spread havoc, signing him up to offensive Web sites, sending viruses, and posting revealing photos. Your child should know not to attempt to resolve any cyber-bullying himself. Once he's told you what's happened, contact the Internet service provider to remove offensive posts, images, or other content. If the offense steps way over the line, you may need to contact local law-enforcement officials.*

Cyber House Rules

Again, you may not be able to control everything your child sees or hears online, but you can set some clear ground rules and employ some basic modes for monitoring his compliance at home.

[1] Set clear limits regarding social networking sites and the specific types of Web sites your teen can visit.

[2] Install blocking and filtering software on your home computer to reduce his contact with unsavory sites, images, and information. Yes, he can find a way around this rule by accessing a computer outside the home, but you will be reducing the temptations.

[3] Use your Internet service providers' parental control settings.

[4] Put all home computers in a central place, such as the kitchen or family room, where you won't be violating your teen's privacy by walking by or pulling up a chair.

DOC TALK: Some parents install monitoring software on the family computer. Keep in mind that doing so is essentially the same as spying on your teenager. Be sure to tell your child that the home computers are wired for security, and that you may be randomly spot-checking their use. If you want to teach your teen trust and honest behavior, you need to model it yourself with full disclosure.

A tip for making Facebook safer: Be sure to set the privacy settings as restrictively as possible. Choose the settings that allows only people you have chosen to access your family members' profiles.

The Birds and the Bees:
It's Time for "The Talk"

Think back on how you learned about sex for the first time. You probably still squirm when you remember how your parents very awkwardly told you the facts about intercourse. It may have been hugely uncomfortable to hear this information from your mom or dad, but it was probably made doubly so because your parents had miscalculated the timing of when to have "the talk." By then, you'd already learned all about it from the kid down the street.

And therein lies the key to the birds and the bees talk. You need to plan on having many mini-conversations with your child throughout the preteen years, based on what's developmentally appropriate for him at a given age. In this way, by the time your child is a teen, he will be familiar with the main issues surrounding sexuality. Returning to the subject frequently gives kids a chance to ask parents questions and to test out theories as they experience the world.

My Body, Myself

A sensible groundwork laid down during the preschool years will help your teen later cultivate a deepening sense of self and control. The conversation for those early years should have included some basic concepts to help her respect her body and understand that she has control over it.

[1] Teach your child to respect her body by eating well and exercising.

[2] Teach her to use the proper anatomical terms for penis, vagina, orgasm, and so forth, so that she can become comfortable talking about sexual topics.

[3] Teach her to be mindful that her body is her own and that it is private.

[4] Teach her that she should not touch others' private parts, and that no one is allowed to touch her private parts. (Initially, you can explain that these are the parts covered by a bathing suit.)

As your child matures, she may begin to show special interest in another child. Some kids begin this around age 8, but typically by age 11 parents will notice it a lot more. By this time, children may start talking about "going out" with another kid, which may just mean they hold hands or kiss or are just regarded by their friends as a pair.

These feelings evolve as kids get older, so be ready to answer their questions. In our sex-laden culture, teachable moments abound.

■ Be alert and ready to respond to your child's natural curiosity.

■ Recognize that movies, television shows, or songs create opportunities for you to explain feelings about sexual behaviors. Even a trip to the zoo where turtles are humping lustily can be a starting point for conversation.

■ Always finish such conversations by encouraging your child to ask you further questions when he thinks of them.

Sex Is the Word

When your child is around nine or ten years old, you can begin to offer more detailed information.

■ You might want to begin by saying, "Let me tell you a little bit about the word 'sex' because you may be hearing it a lot these days." Just have a brief, two-minute conversation to start.

■ Tell your child that sex happens between two people who care about each other, and that both people have to be equally willing. No one should feel forced to be sexual.

■ As your child begins to express interest and ask questions, you can get into the mechanics of how sexual intercourse works.

■ Remember that sex includes not only vaginal intercourse but oral sex and hand sex as well.

EXPERT TIP: *A lot of parents wonder about the degree to which they should be candid about their own sex lives. How you contend with this issue depends on your individual comfort level, but by not revealing a lot of details, you are reinforcing the concept of privacy and intimacy, which is 100 percent okay. Most kids would really rather not know what their parents are doing between the sheets, anyway.*

If your child has not expressed any curiosity about sex by age nine, you can start a discussion by asking, "Do you have any questions about how babies are made?" You can also give her a conversation opening by suggesting you read a book on the subject together. Having you both focus on the page can be less embarrassing than a face-to-face conversation. Even if she opens the book and quickly says, "Mom, are you kidding me?" it will still get the conversation going.

STDs Are Scary, and Other Serious Topics

Once your teen knows that babies don't get dropped into a bassinet by a stork, and once he becomes more emotionally mature (usually between the ages of 14 and 16), the conversation can evolve to cover more sophisticated subjects, including feelings and conditions of readiness for intercourse, sexually transmitted diseases, pregnancy, safe-sex protection, and even rape and date rape. It might be useful to introduce these topics by talking about newspaper or magazine articles you've read. Speaking about hypothetical situations can be an easier way for you both to hash out opinions and emotions on potentially embarrassing subjects.

Risk Management

As a parent, you no doubt want your child to wait to have sex (if he has to have sex at all) at least until he is emotionally mature and has found a special partner with whom he has a deep connection and a mutually satisfying relationship. Sex is a positive thing when the conditions are right. But a couple needs to be mature enough to make a joint decision to engage in sexual activity of their free will while still having their wits about them to take appropriate precautions and stay safe.

So how do you deliver such a qualified, complex message to a teen whose judgment is mostly spotty and whose hormones are in overdrive? Get used to it. You're going to need to hammer away at some scary facts so that your child develops an inner voice to protect against impulsive, imprudent forays into the world of sex before he's ready. Be sure to use "I" statements to send this message, as in: "The risks of STDs are pretty scary. I'm worried about you."

When delivering the facts about sexually transmitted diseases, be sure to note:

■ There are six types of STDs, and only a few of these can be cured with antibiotics. The rest are viral and cannot be cured; they can only be managed when there's an outbreak.

■ Type 2 (genital) herpes is probably a lifelong condition, and it, too, cannot be cured.

DOC TALK: The more accurate label for an STD is "STI" or "sexually transmitted infection." The distinction is important: You can have an infection (e.g., HIV) but not necessarily the disease related to the infection (AIDS). Your child may want to blow off the statistics, but these are the facts:

■ *Teens (ages 15–19) have the highest rates of STIs compared to any other age group.*

■ *50 percent of all new AIDS cases diagnosed today occur in individuals younger than 25.*

■ *The most common symptom of an STI is nothing: no smell, no bump, no discharge. Not having symptoms does not mean you're in the clear.*

■ *The incubation period for STIs can be days, weeks, or months.*

Protection, Protection, Protection

Your values, religious beliefs, and practicalities of life will all play into what you want to communicate to your child about birth control, measures for safe sex, and abstinence. It's a personal choice each family makes. Yet all parents want their children to be out of harm's way and free from disease.

Open conversations and accurate information go a long way toward keeping children safe. You may consider accompanying your child to get birth control so she can feel confident about what she is doing. Request a private meeting with the pediatrician if you need guidance on this issue.

DOC TALK: *When do girls need to see the gynecologist? When she fits any one of these criteria: she turns 16–21 years old; she is sexually active; she has problems with her periods. We recommend girls start breast self-exams at 18 years (instructed by their pediatrician or family provider), but girls do not need a pap smear until they've been sexually active for a few years. Your doctor should check your daughter for sexually transmitted diseases with a simple urine specimen or vaginal swab. Boys should be screened for STDs at their physicals; this can easily be done with a visual inspection and a urine specimen.*

The Changing Ways of Love

The ideas of courtship and dating you grew up with have evolved dramatically over the years. Yes, there are still those boys and girls who pair off for heavy petting at the movies and are as committed to each other as old married couples. But a more recent trend that a lot of parents find disturbing is "hooking up." Not familiar with the phrase? Well, it's broadly defined as pairing off for a casual, no-strings-attached connection that can involve anything from kissing to oral sex (which many kids don't regard as sex because of the lack of penetration).

Be aware: Depression and sexually transmitted diseases are not uncommon results of these impromptu sexual encounters.

How to Be an Understanding Parent

Sexual experimentation starts during the teen years for many kids, but not all. Some kids don't date in high school and don't want to have sex. Many feel they are too young. For some it goes as far as kissing; for others, it's sexual intercourse.

As a parent, you need to reiterate the core values about sex you've been teaching all along.

■ The decision to have sex should be mutual for both people involved.
■ The couple should come to the exchange willingly and with respect for each other.
■ The couple should see sex as a way to feel closer.
■ Neither person should use sex or sexual interactions as a way to seek attention or to bolster shaky self-esteem.

Yes, double standards still apply today, just as in your day. Girls still get labeled "slutty" and diminish in reputation, whereas boys often gain stature among peers for the same behaviors. But make it clear to your child that neither part of a couple "wins" when they have sex without an emotional connection.

[1] **Make like Socrates.** Help your teen think about these issues with some candid conversations. Find out what your teen knows, and then start your Socratic dialogue: Guide him with some open-ended questions that will get him thinking about the consequences of risky behavior. Ask, "Do you have any questions about sexuality?" or "Are any of your friends doing anything you are troubled about?" Teens are less likely to open up to judgmental parents. If you want your teen to speak comfortably about these sensitive subjects, he has to see and hear you act and speak with an open mind.

[2] **Set some rules.** Children are often glad to have these rules in place. It gets them off the hook with their peers if they can say, "Mom will kill me if I ____." Even his friends will respect this. Be open to being the "bad guy" so he can blame you and escape peer pressure or risky situations.

[3] **Role-play.** Ask your teen about parties or places where she sees risky behaviors. Use some improv role-playing to have her try out responses for situations in which she might feel pressured to do things she doesn't want to do. You can teach words of empowerment such as: "Respect me, respect my choice," and, "When I said NO, I meant no."

[4] **Hop on the Straight Talk Express.** Acknowledge that your son probably feels horny a lot. Talk about his urges for intimacy. You can help him figure out ways to channel his feelings so that the target of his attention won't get hurt emotionally or be pressured physically. Make sure he knows that sex is not the only way a boy can feel close to someone.

[5] **Talk about the freedom to choose.** Teens of both sexes need to be reminded that they have the right to choose whether to have intercourse; that a person's body is precious and should be respected; and that intimacy should be reciprocal. If oral sex is happening among your daughter's friends, ask her if it's primarily girls going down on boys and not vice versa. Ask her why boys often don't want to kiss the girls who are servicing them. Ask her if she thinks that seems right. Appeal to her sense of fairness and justice.

[6] **Remind your teen that situations can get out of control.** Discuss the powerful role of alcohol in clouding judgment and disinhibiting behavior. You can role-play ways to say "no" in situations that are getting out of control. Teach your child to say, "Let's slow down now."

[7] **Remind your teen about the repercussions of unprotected sex.** Make sure she has accurate information about pregnancy and sexually transmitted diseases and how they are passed.

[8] **Talk with other parents.** Know the culture of your child's school. If other parents share specific concerns, you can spur the school to hold workshops for teens and parents on subjects pertaining to sex and sexuality.

⊕ *DOC TALK: You may wonder whether allowing your teen access to condoms and birth control sends the message that you're giving your approval to her having sex. Research has shown, however, that parental involvement in making sure children know how to protect themselves sends the message that you want them to be as safe as possible. It's not a free ticket to let her do as she pleases, but rather to know the repercussions of sexual behavior.*

Is My Teen Gay?

How's your gay-dar? In-tune parents usually know—or at least have an inkling—that their child is gay, but not always.

Typically, boys "come out" sooner than girls. Because females often have close and intense emotional and physical relationships with other girls in a way that is generally accepted as heterosexual, they may not be as quick to confront the difference in their sexual orientation. Boys, however, can't have such closeness with other boys and still be regarded as "straight." They're forced to come to terms with their sexual identity sooner. Even as teens and young adults come around to the possibility they may be gay, many initially self-identify as bisexual. The half commitment can be more manageable emotionally as they transition into gay acceptance.

If you think your child is gay, you need to create a safe haven for him or her to talk over feelings. Many times kids are worried about their parents' reaction. You can make a point to identify gay friends, parents, colleagues, and celebrities to normalize the concept.

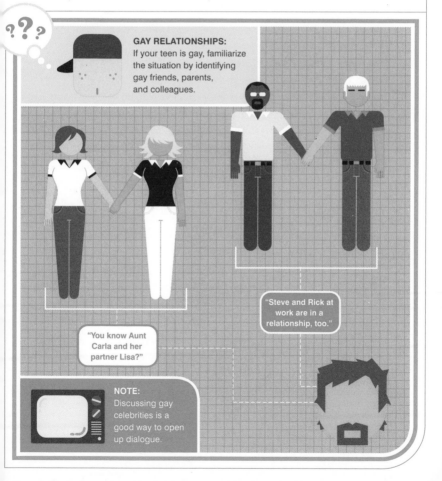

■ You can ask, "Have you ever wondered about sexual feelings or sexuality?" This open-ended type of question gives room for your child to verbalize and address feelings, confusion, doubts, or worries.

■ Reassure your child that, whatever he discovers about himself, you love and support him. If your teen initially denies being gay, revisit the question later. Many gay teens deny their identity at first, worried that an honest answer will have negative consequences.

■ If your teen comes out, your role as a parent is to inform and prepare your child with accurate information about the risks of sexual relationships, just as you would for a heterosexual child. In addition, however, you also have to warn about the risks of violence from people who are uncomfortable around gay people. It's not okay for anyone to bully, harass, or be physically violent toward any gay person, and your child needs to know that you will always step in to make sure he or she remains safe, whatever the circumstance.

■ Parents of gay teens (or teens who are struggling to figure out their orientation) need to be watchful for signs of depression. Your child may be at more risk for depression and suicide while wrestling with emotions and identity in a world in which homosexuality is not universally accepted.

■ Parents who are worried and uncomfortable about their child being gay should seek counseling so they can understand their own feelings. You can seek support and information at PFLAG (Parents and Friends of Lesbians and Gays) or similar organizations.

■ If your child's school does not have outreach programs that promote acceptance, safety, and understanding of gay students, contact a local Gay/Straight Alliance for support and advice on starting one.

Breaking Up Is Hard to Do

Usually in middle or late adolescence, your teen will have her first serious relationship and then endure its breakup. She's in for some serious suffering of the heart, especially if this is the first time she's fallen in love. Your child's identity had become intertwined with another person's, and suddenly the relationship is severed. The teen is adrift, does not know how life can go on, and doesn't have the life experience to know that her heart will mend. Some kids even express suicidal thoughts or become particularly reckless.

Help your child get through the worst of heartache:

[1] Think of your teen as a child for the moment. She may be sobbing, not thinking straight, and far from the poised young lady she usually is. Many teens regress due to the stress of a breakup. Make soup for her and treat her to her favorite magazines or foods. Put some flowers in her room. She needs to be handled gently and to feel safe.

[2] Listen. She may want to talk and rehash the events. She may be confused and blindsided by the turn of events that led up to the breakup. Be a sympathetic listener. Don't try to solve any problems or speculate over what went wrong. Just listen and acknowledge her hurt.

[3] Remind her about who she really is. She is still the same person she was before dating that guy. Talk about the things she likes to do: favorite hobbies, movies, and memories. These are subtle but important reminders that she is a whole person despite the breakup.

[4] Give her a change of scenery. If she loves theater, whisk her away to the nearest city for a night out on the town. She may be miserable and

morose throughout the night, but it may help to see people out in the world, and she may surprise herself by getting engaged in her surroundings.

[5] Ease the fear. She may be worried about how she can return to school after the breakup. "How can I sit in class with him there?" or "What if I see him holding hands with another girl?" Make the unknown more known by role-playing what she could do in these scenarios.

EXPERT TIP: Be aware! If you're worried your teen may harm herself, drop whatever you are doing and start talking to her. Ask, "Have you thought about not living or wanting to go to sleep and not wake up?" You must take immediate action if she has the thought, intent, and plan for suicide. Seek professional help at once.

Here are some tips on how to help your teen get through a rough breakup:

1. Introduce a change of scenery, like a show at the theater, to get her mind off things.

2. Give her some fresh flowers to brighten up her day.

Dance Fever:
Dances, Proms, and Other Courtship Rituals

If you have fond memories of rocking the zombie routine from Michael Jackson's "Thriller," experiencing the thrill of dancing in unison to the hustle, or wowing friends with your disco moves à la John Travolta, well, get ready to do a spit take at the refreshment table when you see what teens are up to at the local boy-girl dance these days.

Not Your Grandfather's Mixer

Schools are trying various ways to guide students away from the eye-popping sexual dance moves, sometimes called "freakin'" or "grinding," that seem to be spreading across the land. If you're a particularly active parent on your child's school social-planning committee, you can use a few of the following strategies to keep things from getting too hot:

■ Suggest the school switch from teacher chaperones to parents or grandparents as chaperones. Blood relations will be more motivated to tone down the dancing. And few kids want their granny watching them get jiggy on someone.

■ Give the DJ an approved song list that isn't conducive to suggestive dance moves.

■ Introduce the "freeze dance" game to break the rhythm of any particularly rambunctious teens.

■ Market the dances as "Trips Back in Time." Teach square dancing or swing dancing, the Mashed Potato, the Pogo, or the Macarena. If the kids are busy trying to master quaint steps from yesteryear, they won't be able to get their hands—and bodies—all over one another on the dance floor.

PROM PROTOCOL

He gives her a **CORSAGE**

She gives him a **BOUTONNIERE**

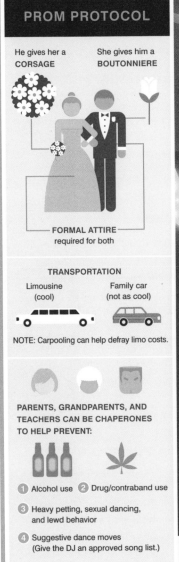

— **FORMAL ATTIRE** —
required for both

TRANSPORTATION

Limousine
(cool)

Family car
(not as cool)

NOTE: Carpooling can help defray limo costs.

PARENTS, GRANDPARENTS, AND TEACHERS CAN BE CHAPERONES TO HELP PREVENT:

1. Alcohol use
2. Drug/contraband use
3. Heavy petting, sexual dancing, and lewd behavior
4. Suggestive dance moves (Give the DJ an approved song list.)

■ Add more socializing possibilities that are sociable but not so sexy. How about school volleyball mixers? or floor hockey tourneys?

■ Pull the plug. If the teens are heedless of chaperones' warnings, simply stop the music and turn on all the lights.

Prom Pointers

Nothing says prom season like tuxedos, slinky gowns, too much make-up and hairspray, too much alcohol, wild dancing, yearned-for or realized sexual encounters, staying up around the clock, and blurry, but happy memories of the whole experience. The allure has not faded. This generation gets just as revved-up about the prom and the after-parties as yours did, though these days kids sometimes forgo dates and just attend in a big group.

Yes, there will be those charming moments of fathers teaching sons how to tie bowties and mothers escorting their daughters to the hair salon to get their updos. But the prom also poses the triple-threat of excess to make a parent's blood run cold. Alcohol, drugs, and sex are topics that every parent must address—if they haven't steadily already—in the weeks leading up to the big event.

■ Make sure to talk to your child about the dangers of drug and alcohol abuse. Dances are notorious places for teens to try to smuggle in contraband.

■ Role-play ways your teen can refuse to partake in risky behaviors yet maintain "coolness."

■ Be sure your teen understands the specific dangers of drinking and driving. Develop a specific game plan to make sure he does not get behind the wheel if he's had alcohol and that he does not get into the car of any other teen who's been drinking. Be sure he knows that he can call you for a guaranteed pick-up.

■ Be clear with your child that he cannot leave with friends in the middle of the dance. If he asks to go to a friend's house before the dance, confirm that there will be parents supervising on the premises.

DOC TALK: *I've heard plenty of people say, "I know my kid is going to drink after the prom; I would rather she drink at my house, where I know she'll be safe." Be aware: Hosting a drinking party for underage teenagers is not only illegal, but it reinforces a belief that teens must have alcohol to have fun. More important, as hosts of this party, you are responsible for the behavior and safety of all of the guests, even after the party is over.*

[Chapter 5]

Language Requirement:

The Importance of Communication

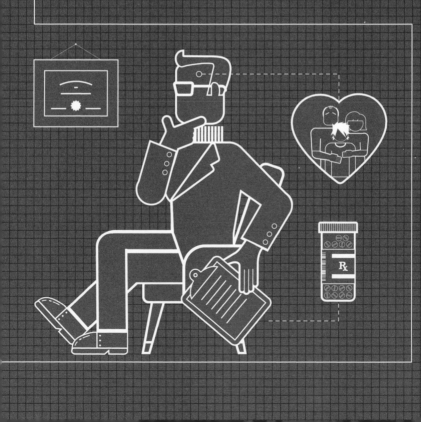

After reading the previous pages, you've already learned that successful communication with a teenager—about sex, crushes, drugs, and even computer-game use—begins with regular discussions in the earliest stages of childhood. But it's never too late too start. If you are respectful, listen without judgment, and are mindful of your teen's growing maturity, she'll likely reciprocate with respect and positive regard for what you have to say. Even though they want to establish their autonomy, many teens still want to please and stay in the good graces of their parents.

Talking Points

The key to good communication lies in knowing what *not* to do and say as much as in what to do and say.

Lectures Don't Work

Make it a point to refrain from any trips down memory lane: "Young man, when I was a teenager . . ." You're not a teenager any longer, and your teen knows this. Anything that follows this preamble will likely be ignored.

Asking questions, rather than giving long-winded lectures, is a better way to plant ideas in a teen's head. It's far more persuasive to arrive at a new point of view through your own mental leaps than when you're simply told what to do. So the next time your teen is mapping out how to handle a tricky situation, ask, "And then what might happen?" This simple question will let her see consequences she otherwise may not have considered.

Be a "Yes" Man

When you show your child genuine curiosity, empathy, and nonjudgmental listening, you'll be astounded at how much detail he'll be willing to share. Say your son reveals to you that he drank at a party last weekend. Instead of a kneejerk response or lecture about underage drinking, you react by saying, "I bet you had some fun with your buddies. What did you like about it?" You will probably hear more on the subject than you ever would have had you delivered your lecture. That's not to say you should try to be "one of the guys" or make a lame attempt at being a "cool parent," but be genuinely curious and realistic about the information your teen is sharing, and in the end you'll have a much better understanding of how to proceed.

■ By acknowledging that your kid might have enjoyed aspects of the risky behavior, you've disarmed him.

■ He might concede that it was fun initially, but the hangover that followed was scary.

■ You can now guide him through the dangers of alcohol consumption, including driving while intoxicated or disinhibition that can lead to risky sexual behaviors.

■ Your teen in turn may feel more comfortable opening up to you and having a thoughtful discussion.

EXPERT TIP: If your teen is laid-back and quiet, he may feel overwhelmed by a parent who is loud, direct, and verbose. Similarly, a chatty teen may not get into a conversational rhythm with a parent who is short on words. Acknowledging your child's different style and attempting to match it to some degree will enhance communications.

Using "I" Statements

When your teen tells you about behavior that might have been shocking or dangerous, your first instinct might be to yell and shout. Teens do some incredibly stupid things. For all these years, you've had control over what she can and can't do, and now that she's striking out on her own, you're left feeling powerless—and worried.

Remember to use your "I"s:

■ An "I" statement is more effective than telling your kid to change a behavior, because it allows room for discussion and an alternate point of view.
■ An "I" statement is hard to counter because your teen can't dispute what's inside your head.

If your daughter wants to go to the mall in a provocative-looking outfit, say, "I worry that outfit makes you look like you're ready for things you're not." Your daughter still has the power to choose what to do, but you've expressed your concerns for her well-being in a non-accusatory way that won't put her on the defensive. It might also encourage her to use similar "I" statements when talking with you and with peers and teachers.

💡 **EXPERT TIP:** *If your child presents you with a scenario, question, or request and you do not have an instant answer, just say so. Responses should not be doled out in the heat of the moment. Kids have a habit of springing requests on parents when they are the most distracted or scatterbrained. Simply tell your teen that you need to think about the question and get back to her. If she insists she needs an answer right away, insist that she will have to wait, or give a "placeholder" response with the clear understanding that you may revise your decision after you've had time to reflect.*

Practice Listening

When teens aren't saying crazy things that cry out for rebuttal, they are often talking about situations that call out for your parental two cents. But beware: You need to practice restraint, or what's called "active listening" in psychology parlance.

■ Resist offering opinions, finishing sentences, and interrupting. Often parents get caught up in the problem and fixing it rather than the simple act of listening to the child vent his emotions and worries. Kids want to share their feelings and have you validate them. They also want to be reassured your relationship can tolerate the strength of their emotions.

■ Wait for the child to open up, and do not pressure him to speak. Your teen needs to speak about something difficult on his own timetable.

■ Don't be hell-bent on getting in the last word.

The No-Gloat Zone

When your child makes a mistake (especially one that resulted from rejecting your advice), refrain from saying "I told you so." Your child actually learns a much more powerful lesson from making a mistake (if no long-lasting consequences come of it) than from having you correct it beforehand. Afterward, you both can talk about how things unfolded and where different choices would have led.

Most teens are aware of just how badly they can screw things up. What your child really needs is your support and some positive words about how things can work differently next time.

How to Deal with Lying

When a parent and a child have a good, trusting relationship, lying and evasion should be minimal. The main thing that promotes lying is when a teen feels that, were he to tell his parents the truth about a situation, he would not be understood, and, worse, be punished. The key, then, is to earn your teen's trust first so that you can expect more truth-telling in return.

■ If you have promised that there will be "no questions asked" when he calls you to be picked up from a dangerous situation, then keep your word.
■ Don't yell or threaten to withhold privileges. If you do, you'll leave the child with little alternative than to lie the next time around.
■ Establish clear house rules and enforce them lovingly and consistently. The result will be less deceit and better communication.

✚ DOC TALK: *For parents, being lied to is the ultimate transgression— the most flagrant disregard of their authority and their rules. For teens, lying is just another way to test boundaries and get what they want. Deal first with the rule that was broken. You can deal with the lying later. In addition, don't take the lying personally; parents who do will often discipline their children less appropriately. Parents feel hurt and angry, and they feel they need to take more extreme measures to extinguish general defiance instead of the specific behavior brought out in this incident.*

When Resistance Seems Futile

When your teen acts out—maybe sneaking off to drink beer or smoke a joint—you need to understand that he's probably feeling ambivalent about his behavior. He knows it's not right, but he's going ahead and doing it anyway. Underneath the tough-guy exterior, however, he's having a slew of conflicting thoughts: "I know I shouldn't be doing this, and I know there are good reasons not to, but I'm doing it anyway because [it's fun/my friends are doing it/I can't think past the moment]."

But the moment your teen hears, "No, you can't do that," the more he may push back, and the balance of ambivalence is tipped toward the negative behavior. A more subtle tactic you can try would sound something like: "I bet there are some good reasons for that. Tell me what you are thinking."

■ If he says drinking feels good, maybe he has some anxiety issues that the alcohol seems to help. Deal with the source of the problem, and the behavior may change.

■ If he says he smokes pot because his friends do, then ask questions about his friends and what he likes most about them. Does he like them for themselves or simply because they've accepted him into their group? Maybe he has self-esteem issues and needs to talk with a counselor.

■ By delving into the problem with genuine curiosity rather than punitive fury, you can discover much more about your teen, his state of mind, and the most helpful form of support he needs.

The Old Silent Treatment?

Often when a teen pulls away, she's simply preoccupied with social life, school commitments, sports practices, and typical teen introspection. Boys tend to retreat more than girls. (Some speculate this is in part hard-wired, along with boys' generally weaker communication skills.)

But when your child becomes completely disengaged from the family, it could be a sign of trouble. Even kids who are highly invested in their friendships will still maintain contact with their families. But a child who has retreated from all communication needs help. Other signs of trouble include sleeping a lot, missing school, changes in diet, failing in school, significant personality changes, binge drinking, or any talk about suicide. Call your child's doctor so you can determine next steps. An appointment with a specialist might be in order.

Communication is key to maintaining connections, but when communications with your teen start to break down, you'll need to develop new ways to keep in touch with his life.

[1] Enforce a regular family mealtime. Sitting around the table and eating together is an ancient ritual that breeds closeness and connections. Your kids have the chance to talk about their days, you have the chance to ask questions, and you all can discuss the day's headlines or upcoming family events. You and your partner also have the chance to model behavior for your children through respectful communication and humor.

[2] Come up with activities you can do together that will get conversation flowing. Instead of walking into your daughter's room and announcing it's time for a talk, ask her to keep you company while you run an errand, shoot hoops, play catch, do yardwork, or just be couch potatoes together. These moments often provide a great starting point for nondefensive communication.

[**3**] Build your information network. Other parents are a great resource for discovering what's going on in your teen's life. They can shed light on situations that your teen may have only alluded to. Talking to other parents can give you information that may diminish your concerns, or you may get news that makes you realize you need to check in with your teen. A parent who informs you about two alcohol-related car crashes that happened over the weekend might move you to have a chat with your son about drinking, designated drivers, and the code words he can use when he's stranded at a booze-soaked party and needs to get home.

Drama Kings and Queens

Why are teens so surly and full of anger? Teens get angry for different reasons: They're overwhelmed, frustrated, sad, hurt, or hormonal. They are emotionally all over the place—far more so than grownups. When a teen comes storming into the house, you frequently need to make a quick assessment. Does she need help de-escalating her emotions, does she need space, or does she need a few sympathetic words?

I Hate You! I Really Hate You!

When a kid gets angry, he may want to talk. He might slam down his books, open the refrigerator, take a look inside, and slam the door in disgust. Start off with an understatement ("You seem like you had a rough day"). Then listen to him unload. By doing so, you're showing that you can tolerate his strong emotions. Provide conversation openers. Once he's talking, you can listen as he vents and then problem-solve when it's appropriate.

But what do you do when the cursing and "I hate you!" screams start to fly? No parent likes to hear this stuff. But believe it or not, it is often

your kid's convoluted way of asking for help. Younger teens, especially, are more likely to say "I hate you" in a fit of frustration.

- Wave away your momentary hurt and try to get to the source of the issue. Parents know the teen does not hate them totally, but more likely hates something specific that happened.
- Say, "It sounds like you're mad at me," and then ask for specifics.
- See if there's anything in what she's saying that you can agree with. If there is, you can use it to break down the oppositional dynamic and get back on the same side.
- Do not shout or curse back at your child.
- Do not give in when the "I hate you" line comes in response to limit-setting. This only reinforces the obnoxious behavior.

The Perils of Profanity

If your child resorts to profanity, remind her of the house rules. Your job is not to be a doormat, but also not to get into a shouting match. Recognize that cursing typically expresses anger that's hiding a deeper hurt—usually something surrounding issues of fairness.

[1] Start off with, "It sounds like you're mad about something."

[2] If your child then says that a teacher gave her detention, you can prompt more conversation with, "It sounds like you are saying that's not fair." This will often open a floodgate of conversation.

[3] Once your child is talking, you have a better chance of giving her the support she needs to handle her emotions. You can say, "I wonder if it hurt

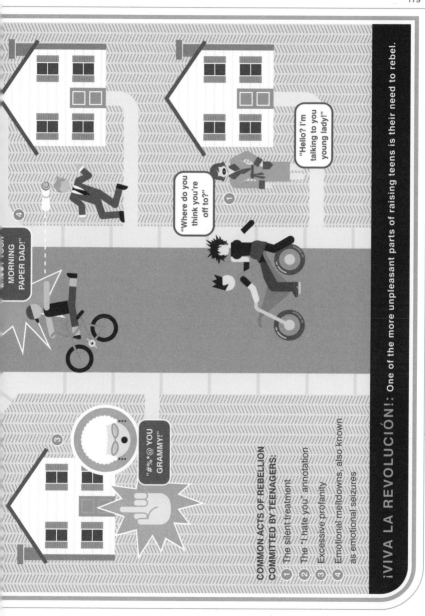

your feelings." Use understatement and observation to help the child put her feelings into real words.

[4] If your teen will not stop using profanity, you can say, "I want to talk with you, but not while you're cursing. Let's talk in an hour." If your child curses repeatedly, you should be prepared to show her concrete consequences, such as removing existing privileges.

Emotional Seizures:
When There's No Going Back

Emotional seizures are usually the points of no return for your teen, when no amount of empathy can steady him—or you. He may need to deplete himself of his anger by shouting, stamping around, and generally communicating to anyone and everyone that he's pissed off. That doesn't mean you have to listen to it, however.

[1] Employ an "I" statement, as in: "I have a hard time listening to you when you're shouting."

[2] Follow up with a specific direction: "Go to your room [shoot some hoops/write in your journal]. We can talk once you've calmed down." This gives both of you time to master your emotions before you try to figure out what just happened. If you don't separate, your teen can use your anger and energy like a hurricane uses water. His anger will feed off your growing emotions and get bigger until neither one of you is fully grounded.

[3] By the time you enter this negative spiral of emotion, it's best to just exit the room, try to steady yourself, and cool down. Slow your breathing,

unclench your fists, relax your face, and drop your shoulders. Now you're modeling ways to regain composure! Too bad your son is too busy hurling school books around his room to notice.

[4] Recognize that while in the middle of an emotional seizure, your teen is incapable of cognitive function. Only afterward will you be able to help him find ways to handle the situation differently the next time.

[5] When you do speak again, encourage him to pinpoint the source of his anger or worry so that you both can gain an understanding of what's causing it. You may also be able to determine whether his anger or irritability may be a symptom of depression. (See page 183.)

EXPERT TIP: *If you get into these skirmishes frequently, plan ahead and practice what to say to yourself before you lose your cool. Remind yourself that your teen isn't destined to be rude forever, and you're not a bad parent just because your teen is going through a rough patch. If you stop thinking negatively, you can stop feeling negative. (With practice, of course.)*

When the F-Bomb Drops:
Take Cover!

Teens are dropping the F-bomb without even blushing these days. Many use it—and other words that would get bleeped on network television—without any shame or thought to those near them. They talk loudly around the elderly, small children, and anyone in earshot.

Cursing and coarse vocabulary pervades teen language, thanks largely to the loosening of cultural standards. For many teens, using "bad" words feels rebellious and exciting at first, as they try to keep up with or outdo their peers. Many kids think they sound older when they use bad language. Later, it simply becomes a habit.

Don't let your child establish the habit to begin with. By the time that happens, the speech patterns will become so entrenched that she won't realize how poorly it reflects on her, or she'll realize it too late, only after the offending phrases or words have passed her lips.

[1] Talk the talk, and set the standards. If you use profanity, so will your child, guaranteed. If you slip up and swear in the heat of the moment, such as in a driving near-miss, apologize to your passengers, acknowledging that the words were offensive.

[2] Teach your kids better words and phrases. Equip them with precise language they can use with pride. If they are looking for verbal power, a well-chosen turn of phrase often has more "punch" than a commonly used expletive.

[3] Break the pattern. Get your child to develop some self-awareness of the habit so that, if she must use the F-word among friends, she can refrain from doing so at Grandma's house. Set up a fine system, in which she loses a quarter for every bad word uttered. Or reward her with later curfews, a bigger allowance, or more gas money when she can go a day or weekend without slipping into old habits.

Moody Blues:
Signs of Teen Depression

As we've learned, it's normal for teens to be more emotional than they were in previous developmental stages. It's also normal for teens to individuate and withdraw from parents. But complete withdrawal is not normal.

There are many factors that can add stress to a teenager's life: academic and social pressures, learning disorders, bullying, divorce, or family problems. Some kids might get down for a short time, but you need to educate yourself to know the difference between temporary blues and a more serious condition that needs professional intervention.

The good news is that most teen mental-health issues are highly treatable, particularly when identified and treated early. Be proactive and make an appointment with your child's pediatrician or school counselor. If your teen resists, tell him that you're setting up the appointment because you want him to talk to someone outside the family, so he can feel entirely free to unburden himself.

Some children are quite secretive about their emotional states. These are often the kids who keenly feel the pressure to be "perfect." Depression and anxiety symptoms can be largely invisible to the casual observer, but the signs include:

■ Extended withdrawal for two weeks or more from family, friends, and interests

■ Change in eating or sleeping habits (too much sleep, nightmares, restless sleep)

■ Change of friends, appearance, and personality

■ Risky behaviors, including sexual activity and substance abuse

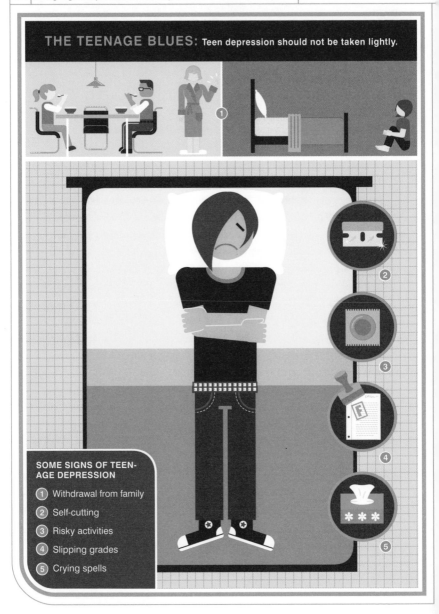

- Lassitude, difficulty concentrating, slipping grades, crying spells, irritability, avoidance of situations, skipping school, nail biting, cutting
- Bodily complaints (including stomach- and headaches)
- Participating in "emo" (emotional) culture, characterized by depressed emotions and cutting

DOC TALK: *For parents, cutting or self-harm is frightening; parents often fear that these behaviors are a signal for possible suicidal thoughts. In general, cutting is about pain: When teens feel intense emotional pain, they may resort to cutting or risky behaviors to displace the pain to their bodies. When teens self-injure, they are not usually thinking about killing themselves. Nevertheless, you should contact your healthcare provider to assess the situation.*

Therapists will often work with parents to improve communication skills and reestablish trust, set and enforce limits and clear rules, and provide structure and routine. Depending on the situation, your child may receive psychotherapy (talking therapy), medicine, or both.

DOC TALK: *What to do/say if your child says, "I will kill myself if—" or "It would be better if I were just dead"? Most important, stop what you are doing. Say calmly, "That is a powerful statement. Please tell me what you are thinking. What do you mean?" Please do not dismiss your teen or tease him. If you are unsure what to do, call your healthcare provider.*

A note about guns: It is estimated that one-third of U.S. households have firearms in the house. Having access to a gun is considered the strongest risk in assessing risk of teen suicide, especially for teenage boys.

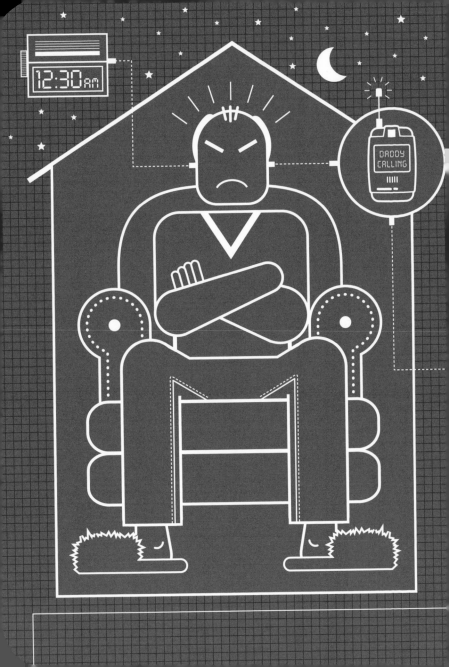

Chapter 6

Pep Rally:

Limit-Testing and Independence

Defiant teens drive parents nuts. Control issues rage. Tempers flare. Accusations fly. Guilt percolates. It's no walk in the park.

Still, all-out teen defiance is rare. Most teens usually go the route of low-level sneaky obfuscation when they want to break rules. ("Oh, did I forget to tell you that although we were meeting at Amy's, we were actually headed over to John's house? I didn't? Oh. Sorry."). Most kids actually do prefer household harmony, but they are also seeking individuation and greater autonomy from their parents. A lot of teens accomplish these tasks relatively smoothly, but some have a bumpier ride. It's your child's job to push for more freedom, more control over choices, and more responsibility. And it's your job to help her achieve this safely.

It all comes down to the fact that you are still responsible for setting limits for your child until she develops enough judgment, maturity, and experience to do it for herself. In the meantime, you want your child to know that you're on the same team. And you want to see that your child has earned your trust and the privileges that come with it.

House Rules and Limits

Your house rules form the foundation from which your teen will operate within the family and the greater world. But it's important that the rules are made explicit.

[1] Start off each school year and summer break with a brief review of the rules for curfews, schoolwork, computer time, driving, chores, and so forth. These rules will change and evolve as your kids get older and wiser.

[2] Discuss the rules with your child so that she can ask questions and you can explain the intention behind them.

[3] Clearly state the repercussions for breaking rules. Be sure that the consequences are logical and appropriate to the infraction.

[4] Make sure to enforce the rules fairly, and with consistent follow-through.

Truth and Consequences

At all costs, avoid improvising punishments for rule-breaking. Creating consequences on the fly or in the heat of the moment will make your decisions seem arbitrary or, worse, the result of momentary anger.

"You cheated on the Chem exam?! You're grounded for the rest of the school year!" This scenario is nearly impossible to enforce because of its extreme duration. What's more, your child will perceive it as punishment for his candidness. Sure, this scenario would be worrisome to any parent. But an angry parent is often a scared parent, and a scared parent may make spur-of-the-moment decisions that are not very well thought out. If you're unsure about how to assign an appropriate consequence, tell your child you need to think it over and that you'll talk to him about it after a little time has passed.

If you've established a guideline already, however, it's merely a case of reiterating the rule and enforcing the consequences for its infraction. For example, if your child comes home past an established curfew, all you need to say is, "I'm sorry you did that. Since you broke your curfew time, you will not be able to borrow the car next weekend."

Some rules are nonnegotiable, such as never drinking and driving and never riding as a passenger with an inebriated driver, but other rules can be negotiated. As your teen earns your respect and trust, she can get more leeway—maybe thirty minutes more curfew time or more minutes on her cell phone plan.

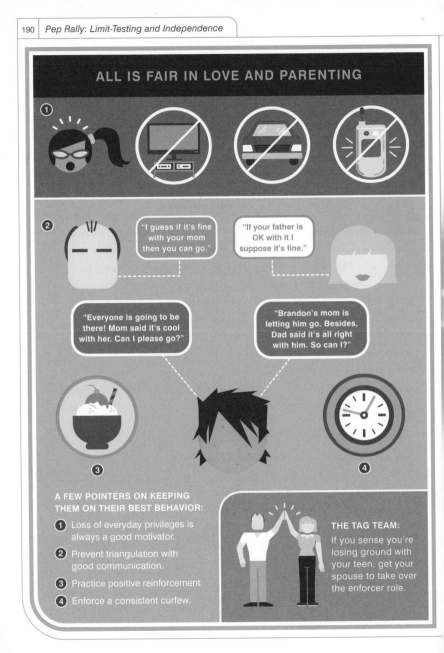

Meet the Enforcer

The most important rule for you to remember is to enforce the limits you've set. If you're haphazard with follow-through, your teen will become confused about the legitimacy of the rules. Keep the list of rules short and simple (nobody can remember a lengthy one), and focus on the nonnegotiable policies that keep your child safe.

■ **Grounding, loss of privileges, and parental disappointment.** For some teens, all it takes for them to do the right thing is the looming specter of parental disappointment. If your child is not as susceptible to the "I'm disappointed" tactic, however, you'll need to sketch out a logical system for withdrawing privileges or grounding to reinforce limits.

■ **Accentuating the positive.** You may want to try a system of positive reinforcement as well, which your child earns rewards for complying with expected behaviors.

■ **Deploying the tag team.** Many teens will pounce on an already-weary parent when they want to change or bend an existing rule or agreement. If you sense you're losing ground, get your spouse to take over the enforcer role. Just don't fall into the same good-cop, bad-cop roles each time.

■ **Avoiding the triangle.** Be alert for the typical triangulation tactics a child can use to play one parent off the other to get what he wants. Check with your spouse to find out what she really said.

■ **Dealing with the great debater.** Teens know their parents' weak spots and will tirelessly work them to their own ends. Stick to your principles, and stick to the topic. Don't let your teen widen the scope of an argument to sidetrack the conversation away from his rule-breaking.

■ **Setting curfews.** Set the time your teen must be home according to her age, her maturity, and any local regulations. Local laws may prohibit teens from driving past a certain hour.

■ **Picking battles.** Be sensitive to temporary circumstances that may require your flexibility. If your son has just had a painful breakup with his girlfriend and he forgot to take out the trash, cut him some slack. You need to be a model for compassion, not just enforcement.

Highs and Lows:
Risks of Substance Abuse

Most parents know that alcohol—particularly binge drinking—will play some role in their teen's social life. Risky behaviors, such as using drugs, sexual activity, and smoking, often piggyback along with drinking. Drug use by teens can go undetected for years before a parent might start to suspect. Many kids will remain in the first stage of experimentation. But not all.

⊕ *DOC TALK: Alcohol is the substance most abused by teenagers and adults. Alcohol is a central nervous depressant—it slows down the brain, impairs vision and coordination, and with excessive use causes unconsciousness and death. The indirect effects of alcohol can be even more profound. Alcohol is involved in almost half of car accident deaths. It contributes to risky sexual behavior, date rape, and poor school performance. Drinking often hides underlying emotional problems of anxiety, depression, and difficulties in school and relationships. So what can we say to our teens about drinking? We tell them that alcohol is a drug and that, with time, they must learn to use this drug responsibly—how to hydrate, how to moderate. But the bottom line is that teenage drinking is illegal. They could get hurt, and they could lose their license.*

Be Prepared

Be sure to prep your kid before she goes out. You will need to talk about the short-term and long-term risks of all of these activities as well as her options for when she's put into difficult situations.

[1] Model responsible behavior when it comes to alcohol and drugs. Your teen's biggest influence is what he witnesses at home. If you overindulge, your child will get the message that he can, too. If you have to have a daily after-work glass of wine or beer, you're sending the message that drinking alcohol is an acceptable way to deal with stress. If your house is always loaded with beer, wine, and hard liquor, you're sending the message that these substances are harmless.

[2] Talk over the risks and attractions of alcohol and drugs. If your teen asks whether you drank or took drugs when they were young, answer truthfully, but keep the conversation directed to your child's reasons for asking. It's a safe bet that he's curious because he's seeing it in his school or social life.

[3] Find out about the substance abuse habits among his friends or at his school. Make sure he knows the legal consequences of underage drinking or substance abuse. Kids should know that, in the United States, most college applications ask potential students if they have ever been found guilty of a misdemeanor, felony, or other crime, and if so, to explain.

[4] Discuss the physical consequences of substance use. Many girls are horrified to discover the calorie content of just one beer. (It's enough to make them teetotalers!) Most teens sober up when they hear what various substances do to a person's brain and other internal systems.

[5] Make rules about party behavior. Give your teen a way to get out of risky situations. Many parents have a "no questions asked" rescue rule. If the child is at a party or in a situation that is over his head, he can call home and be picked up immediately, without having to explain.

[6] Make the last words she hears from you before she goes out something along the lines of: "You're smart. I know you will make good choices. Feel free to call me if you need to." These words again reaffirm your house rules: "I know where you are, I trust that you will be safe, and you can come to me at any time."

[7] Make sure your teen checks in with you face-to-face when she comes home for the night—no matter how late. Knowing you're up and waiting—and ready to smell for alcohol or cigarettes—will curb a lot of bad behavior.

[8] Know the warning signs that your teen might be developing a substance abuse problem: stealing alcohol or money from home, breaking curfew, refusing to introduce new friends to you, jettisoning her old life by skipping school, earning bad grades, dropping extracurricular activities, and taking on defensive and secretive attitudes.

EXPERT TIP: *Some parents offer to call their child at an arranged time for a rescue check-in. If the teen is uncomfortable in a situation, he can explain that his parents have called to hassle him, and that he has to leave. You play the part of the "bad guy" to allow your teen to save face.*

Another way to keep your teen honest is to say that you will be calling the landline of the home where your child will be. (If he is where he's said he'll be, he has nothing to worry about.) If nothing else, you'll have the chance to chat and connect with another parent.

How to Save Face While Just Saying No

Some kids do not want to experiment with drugs, alcohol, or sex. (At least for now.) But even once they know all the risks and consequences, they still must have the gumption to refuse offers while surrounded by peers. Here are some ideas for helping your teen stick to his or her guns, save face, and still feel a part of the social scene.

■ She can simply say, "No thanks. I'm good." Kids will respect her casual assuredness. If pressed further she can say, "It's my choice" or "Maybe later."

■ When told, "C'mon, relax. Everyone is doing it," she can respond calmly with, "No, thanks. I like to be different." Or simply call the cliché for what it is: "You're not actually using that line on me, are you?"

■ Have her blame the parents: "My parents will kill me. I just can't." Or, "My parents will know. They always wait up for me." Believe it or not, kids respect the notion that parents are tough and vigilant.

■ Have her excuse herself to the bathroom to phone or text home. She can explain the situation and say she needs to be picked up right away. If she's concerned about being overheard and perceived as uncool, she can use a prearranged code word or phrase, "Hi Mom, How's the cat doing? Oh, not good? Could you come get me?"

■ Tell her to plead an oncoming migraine or a stomach virus, or to say she's the designated driver.

■ Have her try some humor. If she's being teased with lines such as, "Are you chicken?" she can say, "Hell, yeah. I don't want to become a junkie and have my teeth fall out. I'll stick to my Red Bull and Doritos, thank you very much!"

■ When offered a cigarette, she can say, "No, thanks. I'm hoping to kiss [crush's name] and I don't want my breath to stink."

■ When offered pot, she can say, "No, thanks. It makes my eyes totally bloodshot."

w key techniques or phrases for rejecting alcohol or drugs.

■ When offered alcohol, she can say, "No, thanks. I'm on antibiotics for the next week." She can also take the drink and dump it in a plant, or it can serve as her "decoy" drink that she carries around the whole evening.

■ Be sure she knows she can always find a friend and say, "I don't feel safe. Let's get out of here."

Car Talk:

Learning the Rules of the Road

Learning how to drive is a teen rite of passage. But if the idea of your child controlling 3,000 pounds of metal roaring down the highway at 65 miles per hour is scary, it should be. Car crashes are the number one cause of death for teens.

And yet, despite your fears, your teen will no doubt get a license and learn how to drive. Contact the appropriate department of motor vehicles to find out what the process entails. Most parents know without a lot of deliberation which one of them is more suited to giving driving instruction. If neither of you is the patient type, look into driving schools where someone who is trained (and extremely calm) can do the work for you.

In the United States, once your child has a learner's permit, she must acquire at least 50 hours of practice or wait six months before attempting the driver's road skills test. Once she's passed, be sure she understands the following:

■ Distraction is one of the greatest hazards for a teen driver. Do not allow your teen to have any teen passengers for the first six months (or even a year). Many parents wait until their teen becomes more experienced before they will allow other kids in the car.

■ Do not allow texting or cell phone calling while driving. Teach your child to pull over to a safe place and call or text only when the car is stopped.

■ Teens (and everyone else in the car for that matter) must use seat belts.

■ Driving after using alcohol or drugs is absolutely forbidden. No exceptions.

■ Do not allow driving while drowsy. Most teens are sleep-deprived. Forbid use of the car until your teen catches up on missed sleep.

■ Restrict night driving. Driving in the dark is more difficult and can be too challenging for inexperienced drivers. If she must join her friends to see the latest blockbuster movie after dark, drive her yourself.

■ Make sure your teen follows all laws. Emphasize "no speeding," in particular. The novelty of driving can sometimes transform your sweet, sensible child into a Danica Patrick or Jeff Gordon—even in the family minivan. Remind her to slow down. She'll get there when she gets there.

⚠ **EXPERT TIP:** *Remember that modeling good driving habits and courtesies will have a big impact on how your teen drives. How about using that "thank you" wave the next time a driver lets you merge? Or putting on your turn signal when changing lanes? It's kinder and safer!*

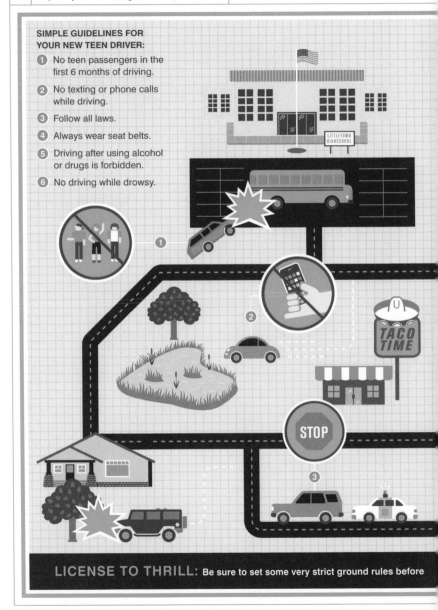

SIMPLE GUIDELINES FOR YOUR NEW TEEN DRIVER:

1. No teen passengers in the first 6 months of driving.
2. No texting or phone calls while driving.
3. Follow all laws.
4. Always wear seat belts.
5. Driving after using alcohol or drugs is forbidden.
6. No driving while drowsy.

LITTLETOWN HIGHSCHOOL

TACO TIME

STOP

LICENSE TO THRILL: Be sure to set some very strict ground rules before

CARL'S GARAGE

u let your teenage son or daughter get behind the wheel.

Money, Work, and Responsibility:
Making Cents

When you were a kid, it felt good to be paid for dog walking, babysitting, lifeguarding at the local pool, or maintaining a paper route. But these days, a lot of teens are in the grips of an overwhelming desire for material possessions. Few are content with what they have. Teaching your child about money and responsibility is an important task at a time when so many children feel entitled to what they have and what they want.

Teens are particularly susceptible to consumer marketing. They want to be like other teens and have all the latest stuff, yet they lack a refined sense of the value of money, a strong ability to delay gratification, or a motivation to save money for a "rainy day."

[1] Guide your child through the basics of money management, including making and maintaining a budget with his allowance money, balancing a checkbook, and saving and investing.

[2] Help your teen set up savings and checking accounts and educate him about the importance of savings versus spending.

[3] Buy a share of a company for your teen and then watch it go up and down on the market together. Pick a stock from a toy company or something that connects to one of his hobbies.

[4] Educate your teen about making financial donations to charities. If he's lucky, he can use dividends from his stock to give to the needy.

A GOOD FIT: Encourage teens to pick a job that suits their personality.

AUTHORITATIVE: LIFEGUARD

QUICK: WAITRESS

ENTHUSIASTIC: RETAIL SALES

ORGANIZED: STOCKER

[5] Establish the rule that chores are not a way to earn money. Your teen must do his chores—whether it's feeding the family cat, taking out the trash and recycling, or mowing the lawn—as a member of the family. Most kids don't mind having some responsibility around the house and like being able to help. (Though many do lock horns with parents over keeping their bedrooms clean.)

[6] If you've decided to give your child an allowance, give it to him at the beginning of the week or month, but refrain from dictating how it is spent and never rescue a kid who has run through this money. No money left to see the latest James Bond film with his buddies? There's always next week with the parents. The idea is to encourage your child to budget wisely since no more money is forthcoming until the following week or month.

[7] Work out what basic costs you will cover (school expenses, clothing needs) versus what your child is expected to pay for.

[8] Credit or debit cards should be given only to teens who are mature enough to handle the responsibility and temptation. Teach your teen about the concept of bad credit as well as the credit card companies' desire to make money off cardholders who carry balances month after month. Some companies offer credit cards that are prepaid by the parent so that a teen can use only as much money as the parent has put on it.

[9] Help your child explore the possibilities of a part-time job. Just make sure the hours don't eat into the precious time he should be devoting to schoolwork or sleep.

Adventures in Teen Style

Teens are using these adolescent years to explore different identities. (Am I a jock, a brainer, a leader, a follower, a party girl, a good guy, a rebel, an activist, a solid citizen, a class clown, Mr. Personality, an alpha-girl, or a free spirit?) They are working their way down the line, picking and choosing what they want.

This is a time when your teen might reject your values, try on new ones, and then return to the original values on his or her own. You can conserve a lot of energy by meeting your teen's new assertiveness with listening, or even enjoying some meaty debates, but not taking things to heart.

Put down the crystal ball and spare yourself the worry that this is all permanent. In fact, it's developmentally healthy for a kid to experiment. Teens who do not experiment might end up delaying part of their maturation process, and it can be a sign that he has taken on a hyper-responsible role in the family that's preventing him from being age-appropriate.

[1] If your teen suddenly adopts a look that you disapprove of, ask him what it is he likes about it or what he thinks he's projecting. Discuss the positives and negatives so that you understand your child's motivations. Perhaps he's adopting the look and mannerisms to identify himself with the music he loves or the personalities he admires.

[2] Be sure he knows to ask your permission before acquiring tattoos or piercings. These permanent changes need parental input ahead of time.

⚠ *EXPERT TIP: Adopting a vegetarian style can be a healthy choice for the sensitive animal lover, but it can also be code for an eating disorder, by giving a child license to overanalyze food and restrict intake.*

COMMON IDENTITIES
TEENS MAY TRY ON:

1 Party Girl
2 Free Spirit
3 Jock
4 Brainiac
5 Activist

MY TEEN HAS MULTIPLE PERSONALITIES: It's both common

healthy for your teen to experiment with different identities and clothing trends.

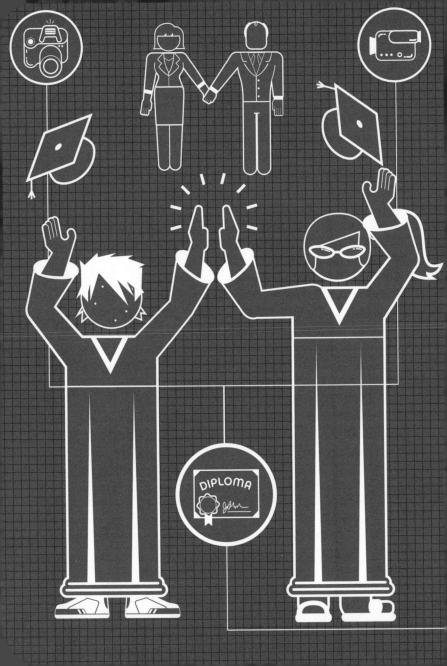

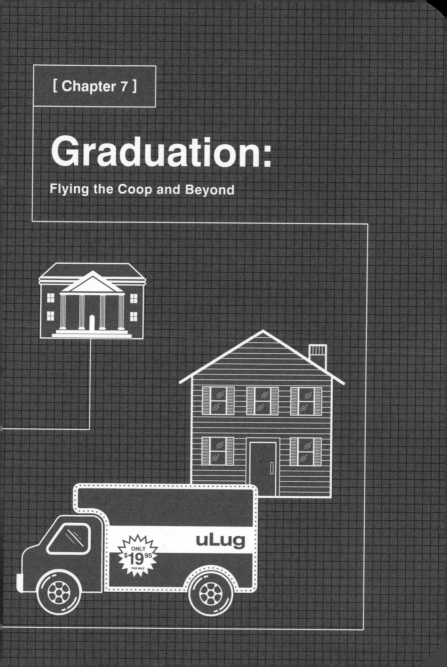

[Chapter 7]

Graduation:

Flying the Coop and Beyond

The first breath our babies draw is the beginning of their long journey of separating from us. It's the way they're able to go forth and build lives for themselves.

You have approximately eighteen years to prepare your kid to leave you. But at the end of that time, you're going to worry:

- Is she independent enough?
- Did you smother him?
- Will she be safe?
- Will he know what to do when tested by forces greater than those he's faced before?
- Is she resilient?
- Does he have high self-esteem?
- Will she have good, healthy, loving relationships?
- Does he have street smarts?
- Does she know how to balance a checkbook?
- Does he know how to do a bleach wash? how long to boil corn on the cob?

There are so many lessons to teach in a relatively short time, but you must have faith that your child is smart and resourceful enough to figure out the challenges along the way by using his unique gifts. Or that he has enough minutes on his cell phone plan to call when he has a question.

Some kids struggle and muddle along, but many others astound us and blossom beyond our greatest expectations into young adults. You don't have a crystal ball to know which way your child will be, but it's likely she'll be a bit of both. The best you can do is to continue to listen and to provide thoughtful words when asked, butt out the rest of the time, and offer constant love and encouragement. Fostering a sense of competence and optimism in your child is important. She will feed off your implicit and explicit messages that you think she's great, smart, responsible, and ready to take on the world.

What to Expect When You're Expecting Your Kid to Leave

It's a huge change for the family when a child leaves home, for siblings as well as parents. Even the family pet will have to get used to the child's absence. Everyone left behind will have to reorganize themselves and form similar but slightly shifted relationships. It can be a difficult period of adjustment.

Here's what to expect:

Emotional bewilderment. You've been pouring so much love, attention, and energy into parenting that you may be emotionally unprepared for this moment. Give yourself permission to feel off-balance for a while.

Tears. Prepare to grieve. Your child is starting a new life, but you still remember the old one so well: her baby years, the first day of kindergarten, the day she learned to swim, the year she got braces, the time she made the soccer team, or the summer she headed off to sleep-away camp. Now your child is almost an adult, and a chapter of your lives is closing. Make sure to have some tissues for the car ride home after dropping your kid off at college.

Euphoria. Some parents are giddy with the possibilities of an empty nest. They promptly redo the child's room into the study, exercise room, or guest room they've always wanted. They refocus their energies on each other as a couple. Others pour newly gained time and energy into careers or fulfilling projects they've never had the time for.

Lack of direction. If you're a stay-at-home parent, especially, you may feel adrift without the anchor of attending to your child, and a lack of purpose may result. Perhaps adopting a puppy or kitten will give you something to focus on. (There's nothing like teaching a rambunctious puppy doggy-manners to consume your attention.) Ideally, though, you will have prepared yourself gradually for this day by beginning to involve yourself in fulfilling work, projects, or hobbies as the teen years progress.

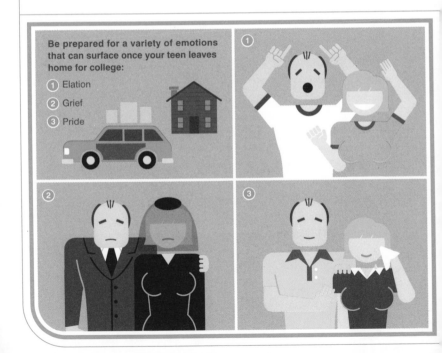

Be prepared for a variety of emotions that can surface once your teen leaves home for college:

1. Elation
2. Grief
3. Pride

Worry. You will never really stop worrying about your child. But though you probably want to set up a sleeping bag in your kid's dorm room, try to give your child space as he strikes out on his own. If possible, wait for him to call home, and try not to wring every last detail out of him about orientation week or his dorm buddies. These are the times to ease up your grip, despite your insatiable curiosity and "need to know."

⊕ *DOC TALK: With cell phones, e-mails, text messaging, and Facebook at their disposal, parents and college kids have much too easy access to one another to allow the child the space to become independent. Resist the temptation to communicate multiple times a day; delay returning a phone call for a few hours or a day; and offer support and encouragement when your child has a problem instead of immediately imposing a possible solution.*

Practical Matters:
The Return

When your college kid returns home for winter break, the summer, or even a long weekend, be prepared for him to expect new freedoms. He's been his own boss during his time away from the family house, so what should the house rules be? It can even be more complicated when siblings who are close in age to your college kid still live at home.

[1] Adapt the rules, but don't abandon them entirely. Yes, he has lived on his own and made his own choices. But no, your house is not the same as a college dorm. If your returning child balks at having rules imposed, make it clear that any person staying at the family home has certain implied or explicit rules to follow. You wouldn't expect your dear Aunt Jane to hole herself up in

the guest room all day studying, then blare music at midnight, head out to a nearby party, and roll back in at 4 A.M.

[2] Be prepared for your child to return—a lot. There's nothing like living away from home to make a kid realize how good he's had it. Many kids who have recently flown the coop come home frequently for home-cooked meals, unconditional love, and access to a washing machine that doesn't gobble up quarters.

[3] Be prepared for your child to return—to stay. The term "boomerang kids" has been coined to describe these co-habitating former teens. Whether for financial reasons or simply for ease, children are returning to their nests in droves, especially during hard economic times and in the period immediately after college graduation. Will this cushy existence undermine her motivation to strike out on her own? Perhaps.

Be sure to talk over all of these issues up front:

■ You and your child should discuss her intentions and your expectations for her return to the family homestead. With an exit strategy, she will be more motivated to get that job, tuck savings away for rent on an apartment, or pay off school loans.

■ Your prodigal child can pay rent and contribute to household costs, pay for her own clothes, do her laundry, and do chores to pitch in with the general upkeep of the house.

■ To spare both parties aggravation and cut down on passive-aggressive gestures, expectations on adult topics such as sex and alcohol should be made clear at the start.

Time to Toss Your Cap in the Air

You did it! You parented your child through the teen years. Hooray! Many parents take great joy in the evolving relationship with their children as they enter early adulthood.

■ Roles shift as you develop more equal terms with your child as an adult.

■ You no longer have to impose limits and expend so much energy to help your child make his way in the world.

■ His prefrontal cortex is either finished forming or nearly there, and his higher-level thinking is making him a heck of lot better conversation partner and all-around companion. (He's also a much safer driver, to boot.)

So sit back and enjoy some moments of contentment. Perhaps you can start preparing for the next phase of life: the delicious pleasures of being a grandparent. You can spoil those little grandkids rotten! You won't need to set any limits, and you can indulge their every last whim and request.

It will be fun providing all the love and none of the limit-setting and discipline. You can leave it all to those children formerly known as teenagers, who are now all grown up.

Once your teens leave home, you can kick back, relax, and celebrate a job well done.

[Appendix]

Index

Acknowledgments

Special thanks to all the parents who helped with the research of this book by sharing their experiences, worries, triumphs, tips, and anecdotes. Also, deep appreciation is extended to all the medical, adolescent, and educational experts who generously shared their time and expertise about all matters of teenage physical, mental, academic, and social development. Thank you to Wanda Anderson, Roger Eastlake, Matt Glendinning, Janice Hillman, Abigail Huntington, Laura Jordan, Armond Lawson, George Preti, Jane Shure, Steve Sokoll, Richard Stern, Craig Stevens, and Judith Turow.

About the Authors

SARAH JORDAN is a National Magazine Award nominated author who has written for magazines and newspapers including *Parents* and *Parenting*. She is the author of *The Pregnancy Instruction Manual* and coauthor of *The Worse-Case Scenario Survival Handbook: Parenting* and *The Worst-Case Scenario Survival Handbook: Weddings*. She lives in Philadelphia with her husband and two children.

JANICE HILLMAN, M.D., FACP, is an adolescent medicine specialist and has been practicing in the University of Pennsylvania Health System for more than 20 years. Named consistently as one of *Philadelphia* magazine's "Top Docs," she frequently lectures to parent and student groups. Dr. Hillman expresses profound gratitude to her family, friends, and patients for their support, confidence, and trust. She cites her greatest achievement, both personally and professionally, as the successful navigation of the teenager years with her two young adult daughters, Jennifer and Abigail.

About the Illustrators

PAUL KEPPLE and SCOTTY REIFSNYDER are better known as the Philadelphia-based studio HEADCASE DESIGN. Their work has been featured in many design and illustration publications, such as *AIGA 365* and *50 Books/50 Covers, American Illustration*, *Communication Arts*, *Graphis*, and *Print*. Paul worked at Running Press book publishers for several years before opening Headcase in 1998. He graduated from the Tyler School of Art, where he now teaches. Scotty is a graduate of Kutztown University and received his M.F.A. from Tyler School of Art, where he had Paul as an instructor.

OWNER'S CERTIFICATE

Congratulations! Now that you've studied all the instructions in this manual, you are fully prepared to maintain your teen. With the proper care and attention, your model will provide you with a lifetime of fun and happiness. Enjoy!

Owner's name

Model's name

Model's date of delivery

Model's gender

Model's eye color

Model's hair color

irreference \ir-'ef-(ə-)rən(t)s\ *n* (2009)

   1 : irreverent reference

   2 : real information that also entertains or amuses

How-Tos. Quizzes. Instructions.
Recipes. Crafts. Jokes.
Trivia. Games. Tricks.
Quotes. Advice. Tips.

Learn something. Or not.

VISIT IRREFERENCE.COM
The New Quirk Books Web Site